AIDS:
TRADING FEARS
FOR FACTS

AIDS:

TRADING

FEARS

FOR FACTS

A Guide for Teens

Karen Hein, M.D., Theresa Foy DiGeronimo,
and the Editors of Consumer Reports Books

CONSUMERS UNION
Mount Vernon, New York

Copyright © 1989 by Karen Hein, M.D., and Theresa Foy DiGeronimo

Published by Consumers Union of United States, Inc., Mount Vernon, New York 10553

Library of Congress Cataloging-in-Publication Data

Hein, Karen.
    AIDS, trading fears for facts : a guide for teens / Karen Hein, Theresa Foy DiGeronimo, and the editors of Consumer Reports Books.
    p. cm.
    Includes index.
    ISBN 0-89043-269-4
    1. AIDS (Disease)   2. Teenagers—Health and hygiene. I. DiGeronimo, Theresa Foy.   II. Consumer Reports Books. III. Title
RC607.A26H45   1989
616.97'92—dc19
                                          89-459
                                          CIP

Design by Binns & Lubin/Martin Lubin

First printing, May 1989
Manufactured in the United States of America

To Ralph, our children, Molly, Ethan, Kenneth, and Laura, and my parents, who come first in my heart even when my mind is immersed in the epidemic

—K. H.

To Mick, for his support and encouragement

—T. D.

Contents

Acknowledgments

Karen Hein would like to thank:

Andrea Orane for helping prepare the resource section, and the rest of the staff of the Adolescent AIDS Program for turning ideas into reality

The young people who have taught me what they need to know and how we can best help them

Admiral James Watkins (Ret.) for his encouragement to do and say what we believe needs to be done

Carole Schaffer, Iris Litt, Dick Brown, and my other friends and colleagues who have kept their perspective even when I have lost my own

Theresa DiGeronimo, Steve Ross, and the Editors at Consumer Reports Books who had the skill, foresight, and courage to create the right book at the right time

Theresa Foy DiGeronimo would like to thank:

Faith Hornby Hamlin for putting this project together

Steve Ross for incessantly asking, "Why?"

All the young people who answered survey questions and shared with us their fears and concerns about AIDS

The men and women with AIDS who gave us their stories and let us peek into their hearts, where we found pain and despair as well as courage and hope

The Editors of Consumer Reports Books would like to thank:

Charlotte Baecher

Bernie Kurman

Introduction: The Story of AIDS Is Not a Movie

Sometimes the AIDS epidemic seems more like a science-fiction movie than medical fact. It has all the ingredients: A plague suddenly appears and kills tens of thousands of people. Doctors are baffled. There is no vaccine and no cure. The disease can hide in the body's cells, so most of the people who have it seem perfectly healthy and show no signs of symptoms at first. They pass it on to other people without even knowing it. Then, as the death toll rises, panic begins to grip the country. To protect themselves, people propose outrageous schemes, like tattooing all infected people or forcing them to live on faraway islands. As the disease spreads, large city hospitals become understaffed and overcrowded. The ill are turned away onto the streets. They've been evicted from their homes and fired from their jobs, so they have no place to live.

If this were a movie, a hero or heroine would probably step in to save the day. But the story of AIDS isn't a movie. It isn't going away. It will be here for many years to come.

Everyone has a part to play in controlling the spread of this epidemic and in helping people who are already infected. The first step is understanding what AIDS is and how it affects you.

Suppose you found out that the person who held this book before you had AIDS. Would you still hold it and read it? Or would you want to throw it away?

Suppose you knew that the person who sat behind you in English class had AIDS. How would you feel when he coughed or sneezed? Would you join a protest group that wanted him to stay at home?

Suppose your best friend told you she had AIDS. Would you still be close friends with her? Or would you start to avoid her?

Within the next few years you will probably know someone who has the virus that causes AIDS. How will you react? It will be hard to know what to do if you don't know the facts about AIDS.

But the facts can be hard to find. AIDS is new and scary. Many people don't want to think or talk about it. Many have their own unanswered questions. And because it's often hard to talk about sex, drugs, and other things, many don't ask what they really want to know.

That's why we've written this book: to give you correct and complete information. This book is for teenagers. It doesn't preach or lecture. It doesn't tell you what's right or wrong. It just gives you the facts to help you sort out your feelings.

No matter where you live, AIDS will affect you and everyone in your family, your school, and your community. You need the facts on how it spreads and how it doesn't. You need to separate facts from myths, so you'll know what's worth worrying about and what isn't.

Laws about AIDS differ from state to state. You need to know your legal rights: What do the laws say about testing teens for the AIDS virus? Does a career choice or vocational program require testing for the AIDS virus?

You will grow up in a society with people who have the virus that causes AIDS. How you treat them will shape the kind of society you'll live in. Will it be a society based on fear and hostility, or one based on knowledge and compassion? The choice is yours.

This book attempts to answer all the questions you may have today. But the future holds the promise of medical advances and new information. The legal aspects of the AIDS epidemic are also changing. So use the resource section "Call for Help" at the back of the book. If you have questions, you can call or write to get the answers.

AIDS *isn't* science fiction. It's a real part of your world. The information in this book can help you trade in your fears for the facts.

1

THE
FACTS
ABOUT
AIDS

In 1981 there were no known cases of AIDS in the United States among people 13 to 21 years old. Seven years later, at the end of 1988, there were more than 800 reported cases. This number is doubling every year. So you need to know about AIDS.

What Is AIDS?

AIDS stands for *a*cquired *i*mmune *d*eficiency *s*yndrome.

These four words explain exactly what AIDS is:

Acquired: You get the AIDS virus from someone else.

Immune Deficiency: The AIDS virus makes your body unable to fight certain infections and diseases.

Syndrome: AIDS results in a number of different illnesses and conditions, which are usually fatal.

ACQUIRED

The word "acquired" (pronounced uh-KWIRED) refers to the fact that AIDS is something you *get*, something you *obtain*. You do not inherit AIDS from your parents the way you inherit the color of your eyes, for example, or the color of your hair. (However, a pregnant woman who is infected with AIDS can pass on to her baby the virus that causes AIDS.)

IMMUNE

The word "immune" (im-YUNE) means "safe" or "protected." If you are immune to something, you are safe from it or protected against it.

There is a system in your body that fights infections and diseases. It is called the immune system. Illnesses like the common cold, the flu, and measles are caused by viruses. It is the job of the immune system to stop any virus and to keep it from multiplying. The immune system does this by producing antibodies. An antibody's job is to eliminate any virus from the body.

DEFICIENCY

"Deficiency" (di-FISH-uhn-see) means "lack" or "shortage." In discussing AIDS, the word "deficiency" goes with the word "immune." A person with AIDS is "immune deficient"—that is, his or her immune system is deficient. It doesn't work as it should to protect the person against infections and diseases.

When the virus that causes AIDS invades the body, it fools the immune system by hiding in healthy cells. Since the body doesn't recognize it as an enemy, the virus gets a head start at reproducing. It usually takes from a few weeks to a few months for the body to manufacture enough antibodies to the AIDS virus to be detected. By that time, the virus has had a chance to get into other cells. The virus can stay hidden for months or even years before actually producing any symptoms of disease; but the virus will continue to multiply. Eventually, part of the immune system will be destroyed or will become so weak that it can no longer defend the body against disease.

SYNDROME

A "syndrome" (SIN-drome) is a group of symptoms or problems. A person with AIDS may develop a variety of symptoms, like those shown in the table on pages 12–13. (But keep in mind when you look at the table that having one or more of these symptoms does not necessarily mean that you have AIDS.)

Jim Anderson/Woodfin Camp

All About Viruses

By the time you're a teenager, you've probably had lots of viruses invade your body.

You've probably caught a cold from someone sitting near you in school. Coughing and sneezing could have spread the cold virus to you. It might have taken a few days or a week for your body's immune system to fight off the cold virus. But it did, and you got well again.

Or you might have gotten chicken pox from your little brother by using the same facecloth he used. It would have taken your body's immune system several weeks to fight off that virus. But it did, and you got well again.

The common cold, the flu, chicken pox, pinkeye, measles, mumps, rubella, herpes, and mononucleosis (MAH-noh-new-clee-OH-sis) are all examples of an illness caused by a virus.

The virus that causes AIDS is known as the *h*uman *i*mmunodeficiency (im-YEW-noh-dih-FISH-un-see) *v*irus, or HIV. Its name means (1) that it is found in humans, (2) that it attacks the immune system, and (3) that it is a virus.

The viruses that cause colds, flu, or chicken pox are passed easily from person to person because the viruses can survive in air, food, and water. They can be spread by coughing, sneezing, touching, sharing food, or using a water fountain. But HIV is different from the other viruses. It *can't* survive in air, food, or water. It can survive only in body fluids. So a person gets, or *acquires*, HIV only by a direct exchange of infected body fluids, like blood or semen.

HIV is also different in the way that the body reacts to it. The body's immune system can fight off most viruses. But HIV destroys part of the immune system, so the immune system can't fight off HIV or other viruses. This gives different infections and diseases an opportunity to get a strong hold on the body. (This is why the diseases that commonly kill people with AIDS are referred to as "opportunistic.")

Cold, flu, and other viruses are attacked and eliminated by the immune system's antibodies. But HIV isn't. Once it invades the body's cells, it stays there for life. Some people die within a couple of years. Most may live five or six years before they actually get symptoms of AIDS. A few have not gotten sick at all so far. But *all* HIV-infected people will probably carry the virus their whole lives.

People who are infected with HIV but have no symptoms of AIDS are "asymptomatic." (The prefix "a" means "without"; "asymptomatic" means "without symptoms.") The graph on page 14 shows that the number of people reported to be *diagnosed* as having AIDS is *much* smaller than the number of people infected with HIV who are asymptomatic. Many infected people don't even know they have the AIDS virus—or that they're passing it on to others. Some know they're infected but don't know if or when they will get symptoms. But research shows that 3 out of 10

Many infected people don't even know they have the AIDS virus—or that they're passing it on to others.

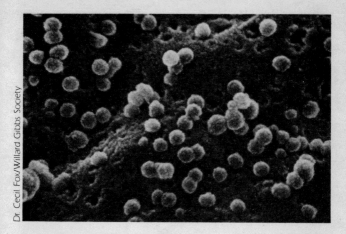

Dr. Cecil Fox/Willard Gibbs Society

The AIDS virus (HIV) budding through an infected blood cell.

will develop AIDS sometime within five years. And 5 out of 10 will develop symptoms of AIDS within seven years of getting the infection.

Signs and Symptoms

The weakened immune system of a person with HIV lets many infections attack the body, so death will actually be caused by a variety of infections or cancers. But there are some common symptoms of an HIV infection. The list that appears on pages 12–13 shows that the symptoms of HIV infection last longer and are usually more severe than those of more common illnesses.

Few people with AIDS have all the possible symptoms at one time. Most have only a few of them. Some people have symptoms that stay for a while and then may disappear, or get worse over time. But even

SIGNS AND SYMPTOMS OF COMMON ILLNESSES	POSSIBLE SYMPTOMS OF HIV INFECTION
Weight loss	Weight loss of more than 10 pounds if you've stopped growing and aren't dieting *or* Failure to gain weight while you're still growing
Fever	An unexplained fever lasting more than a week *or* A very high fever (over 103°) for more than three to five days
Diarrhea	Frequent or loose stools for weeks at a time
White discharge in mouth, vagina, or rectum (called "monilia fungus infection"). This sometimes appears after using antibiotics while on birth-control pills, or in a person with diabetes.	Painful or thick whitish coating in the mouth, vagina, or rectum with no apparent cause or reason
Tiredness when you're busy or when you're not getting enough sleep or when you're experiencing lots of changes in your life or when you have a lot on your mind	Tiredness or weakness that lasts for weeks even when you're getting enough sleep or when nothing out of the ordinary is happening

SIGNS AND SYMPTOMS OF COMMON ILLNESSES	POSSIBLE SYMPTOMS OF HIV INFECTION
Virus infections such as a cold, the flu, or mononucleosis	Many infections each year that last more than three to five days at a time
Swollen glands	Swollen glands in more than one location without other symptoms (like a sore throat)
	or
	Lymph nodes anywhere in the body that are walnut-size or larger
Cough with a cold or allergy	A dry cough or a cough that brings up fluid or sputum from the lungs that lasts for several weeks without explanation
or	
A smoker's cough	
or	
A cough after the flu	
Rashes or itchy skin from contact with plants or chemicals	Unexplained purplish patches that don't go away
or	*or*
Skin disease like impetigo	Extremely itchy or flaking skin with no apparent cause (like poison ivy)
	or
	Sores and infections that won't go away even with medical treatment

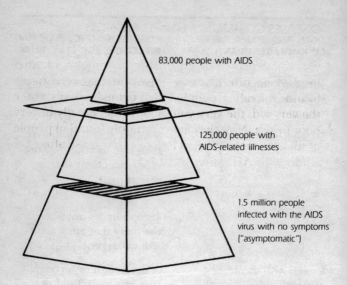

83,000 people with AIDS

125,000 people with
AIDS-related illnesses

1.5 million people
infected with the AIDS
virus with no symptoms
("asymptomatic")

AIDS is a hidden epidemic. The 83,000 cases of full-blown
AIDS reported by the end of 1988 are only the "tip of the
iceberg." Medical experts believe that for every person with
full-blown AIDS, there are between 30 and 50 people with
the AIDS virus. Eventually, 90 percent or more of those people
infected with the virus will develop AIDS. Many of these
people don't know they have the virus—or that they're
passing it on to others.

when the symptoms disappear, they usually return to
cause severe illness or death later on.

You've probably experienced some of these symptoms for days at a time. But there is a big difference
between the symptoms you've had and the symptoms
caused by HIV: with HIV the symptoms drag on for
weeks or even months. HIV stays in your body
whether you feel sick or not. An infected person
never completely recovers.

DISEASES COMMONLY LINKED TO AIDS

Within one or two years after getting the HIV infection, most people begin to show symptoms of what used to be rare diseases—diseases that were rarely found in healthy people. They would usually strike the very old, the very young, or those already in very poor health. Now they are commonly found in people of all ages with AIDS. The ones that most often kill adults with AIDS are:

1. Kaposi's sarcoma (kap-oh-SEEZ sar-KOH-muh), a form of cancer that appears as purple blotches on the skin

2. Pneumocystis carinii (new-moh-SIS-tis kuh-RIN-ee), a rare infection that usually settles in the lungs and causes pneumonia

3. Lymphoma (lim-FOH-muh), a rare cancer that sometimes starts in the brain

People with AIDS are also more likely to get mononucleosis (mono), tuberculosis (TB), syphilis, and other infections. The symptoms are usually more severe, last longer, and are more difficult to treat than with people who don't have AIDS.

The Ways You Can Get the AIDS Virus

It is not easy to get the virus that causes AIDS. HIV can enter the bloodstream when it's injected with other substances, or it can infect cells in the rectum and vagina directly. In both cases, it has to come into *direct* contact with the blood or cells.

It is not easy to get the virus that causes AIDS.

The four most common ways HIV passes from one person to another are:

→ Sexual intercourse with an infected person

→ In needles or syringes used by an infected person

→ During pregnancy, birth, or possibly while breast-feeding, if the mother is infected

→ Transfusion of infected blood or blood products, or organ transplants before 1985.

When AIDS first hit the news in the early 1980s, it seemed to be infecting only three groups of people: male homosexuals, IV drug users (drug users who inject drugs directly into their bodies with needles and syringes), and people who had received blood transfusions. So, many people not in these groups thought they weren't in danger. But that isn't true. You can get the AIDS virus if you have sexual intercourse with *anyone* who has been infected with HIV. That includes an infected drug user, a bisexual person (someone who has sex with both men and women), a heterosexual person (someone who has sex only with the opposite sex), or even someone who contracted HIV through a blood transfusion or an organ transplant.

Dan was a 21-year-old carpenter when he met 20-year-old Marcy. After a year of dating they got married, and the following year they had a baby girl. Two

AIDS.
It takes all kinds.

Judy Thompson
1941-1986

Mallory McCarthy
1968-1985

Christopher Rubin
1984-1986

AIDS is caused by the same thing that causes many illnesses.
A virus.
And, like any other virus, the AIDS virus doesn't care whether you're male or female, gay or straight, young or old. All it cares about is finding a nice, warm body to destroy.
So the sooner you accept the fact that AIDS is not someone else's problem, the sooner it won't be yours.

AIDS ACTION
C O M M I T T E E
661 Boylston Street, Boston, MA 02116
1-800-235-2331

Wide World

years later the baby died of AIDS. Dan and Marcy were angry and confused because they thought only homosexuals and intravenous (IV) drug users got AIDS. Dan had never had sex with another man. Neither Dan nor Marcy had ever used intravenous drugs. Both of them were in good health. So how could this have happened to their baby? After months of searching, they finally found the answer in Dan's past. When he was 16, he had had sex with a girl who had gotten HIV from a boyfriend who was an IV drug user. She unknowingly passed the HIV infection on to Dan. But Dan didn't know it, because he had no symptoms. He then passed it on to Marcy when they had sexual intercourse, and she passed it on to the baby. Today Dan and Marcy know that AIDS is not just for a few groups. They know that *anyone* can get it.

Children, teenagers, and adults can all get the AIDS virus through sexual intercourse and IV drug use. But each age group has to worry more about certain methods of getting it. IV drug use, for example, is a more common source for teens than for adults. Also, more teenage girls than adults get AIDS from sexual intercourse. Twenty-nine out of every 100 adult women with AIDS got it from sexual intercourse, but 50 out of every 100 teenage girls with AIDS got it from sexual intercourse.

Men have to worry about AIDS more than women. Across the nation, 13 adult males have AIDS for every adult female with it. But *teenage* girls aren't as safe. With teens, only 7 boys have AIDS for every girl with it. In New York City, for every 3 boys with AIDS, 1 girl has it. Some researchers are afraid that HIV infection could become as common in teens as syphilis, gonorrhea, herpes, and other sexually transmitted diseases. It could affect just as many females as males, as it now does in Africa. When this happens, the number of AIDS cases could quickly rise among teenagers who have intercourse.

Even teens who haven't had sexual intercourse may be at risk. Some may have been infected by transfusions of infected blood for hemophilia (hee-moh-FEE-lee-uh), sickle-cell disease, or other illnesses. Teens who needed many transfusions while they were

Wide World

In August 1987, Olympic gold medal diver Greg Louganis gave the gold medal he'd just won in the Pan American Games to 16-year-old Ryan White, an Indiana teenager with AIDS.

growing up in the 1970s and early 1980s (before tests for HIV were available) may now carry HIV. If they have sexual intercourse without using safer-sex practices (described in Chapter 2), the number of infected teens will continue to rise rapidly.

Unlike adolescents, most children with HIV got it from their mothers, who were either infected IV drug users themselves or the sex partners of IV drug users. And unlike older people with the AIDS virus, children get sick much sooner (usually within a few months), and they die earlier (usually within two years). Even common infections that are usually easy to treat, like pneumonia, can kill them.

There's also a group of people who don't know how they got the virus. They may have been infected by people who didn't know they had the virus. Or they may engage in more than one risky behavior—both homosexual intercourse and IV drug use, for instance. Or they might not want to admit to having sex with people of the same sex or to being an IV drug user.

The Ways You *Can't* Get the AIDS Virus

The AIDS virus doesn't spread through day-to-day casual contact, *because HIV cannot survive in air, or water, or on things people touch*. So there's no reason to fear being near people with AIDS. HIV survives only in the blood, tissues, and some body fluids of infected people. It spreads only if those infected fluids get into the blood or body tissues of another person. That *doesn't* happen by touching them. Even if infected people sneeze or cough around you, you aren't in danger, simply because you have not taken their blood or body fluids into your body.

We're lucky the AIDS virus is so different from the viruses that cause the flu, chicken pox, and measles. Unlike HIV, they spread easily because they live in saliva, mucus, and tears or on the skin. They can survive outside the body, in water, on food, in the air, and even on doorknobs, telephones, and drinking glasses. One way you can avoid getting *those* viruses is by avoiding people who have them and by not sharing their toothbrushes, tissues, and washcloths.

But HIV (the virus that causes AIDS) is not at all like these viruses. No friends, teachers, coworkers, or

AIDS doesn't spread through day-to-day casual contact, because HIV cannot survive in air, or water, or on things people touch.

classmates of any person with AIDS ever got the AIDS virus unless they had sexual intercourse with them, shared IV needles with them, or had lots of contact with their body fluids. Eight studies were conducted of 500 people who lived with people with AIDS. The 500 people shared toilets, toothbrushes, dishes, bed linens, and towels with the people who had AIDS. But not one single person got the AIDS virus. These studies show that:

1. The AIDS virus does *not* spread through contact with unbroken skin, and it does *not* survive outside the body, so you can't get it by:

→ touching

→ hugging

→ holding hands

→ dancing

→ shaking hands

→ sitting on toilet seats

→ eating food prepared by people with HIV or AIDS

→ any other form of casual contact

2. The AIDS virus does *not* spread through things we touch each day, so you can't get it by touching things like:

→ gym equipment

→ telephones

→ headphones

→ typewriters

→ towels

→ money

→ doorknobs

→ handrails

→ anything else that may have been touched by someone with HIV or AIDS

3. The AIDS virus has never been transmitted by:

→ sharing a sandwich, soda, or cigarette

→ using the same dishes, forks, spoons, or coffee mugs

→ being spit, drooled, or cried on

→ using a public water fountain

Much of the fear of AIDS comes from not understanding these facts. There have been stories in the news about parents who wouldn't let their children go to school with kids who have AIDS. People have refused to eat in restaurants that hire homosexual cooks or waiters. A town shut down its public swimming pool when a person with AIDS went swimming. Some

Wide World

Clifford and Louise Ray with their three sons: Ricky (11 years old), Robert (10 years old), and Randy (9 years old) in Florida. All three boys are hemophiliacs who got HIV through transfusions. In 1986, school officials in De Soto County, Florida, where the Rays lived, said the boys could not attend class with other children for fear they might spread the AIDS virus. In August 1987, a United States District Court judge ordered the school to allow the Ray brothers to attend school. Four days after the boys started school, their house was burned down in a suspicious fire. The family then moved to Sarasota County, 50 miles away, where the boys attend school. In September 1988, the De Soto County school district agreed to pay the family $1.1 million for not letting the boys attend school. Mrs. Ray says she hopes school officials "have learned as much from this situation as we have. You shouldn't be afraid of someone who has AIDS because you can't catch it. And if you have a disease, you shouldn't have to be ashamed of it."

landlords have evicted people with AIDS from their apartments. These people probably think that HIV can spread like a cold virus. But they're wrong. It can't.

If the AIDS Virus Is Hard to Get, What's the Big Deal?

The AIDS virus *is* hard to get—*unless you have sexual intercourse or share a needle and syringe with an infected person*. That must be happening frequently, however, because the AIDS virus is spreading very quickly to many people. The number of reported AIDS cases in the United States will probably grow from 83,000 at the end of 1988 to 270,000 by the end of 1991, and to 450,000 by the end of 1993.

These numbers are especially frightening because the disease is relatively new. The early cases (in the late 1970s) were in New York City and San Francisco. The first people with AIDS lived mostly in large cities. But today people everywhere can have the virus.

There have been stories in the news about parents who wouldn't let their children go to school with kids who have AIDS. These people probably think that HIV can spread like a cold virus. But they're wrong. It can't.

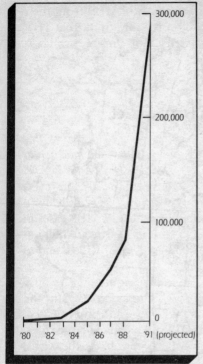

The rapid spread of AIDS. In the spring of 1981, the first five people were diagnosed with AIDS. By the end of 1988, 83,000 people had been diagnosed with AIDS. This number is expected to rise to 270,000 by the end of 1991. (*Source:* Centers for Disease Control)

They may live in large or small cities or in rural areas. By 1991, 8 out of every 10 AIDS cases may be located outside the big cities where the first cases were reported.

One reason why the number of AIDS cases will continue to grow is that many people infected with HIV don't have any signs or symptoms. They spread the virus without knowing it. Many people who were infected in the 1970s and 1980s are just beginning to get symptoms.

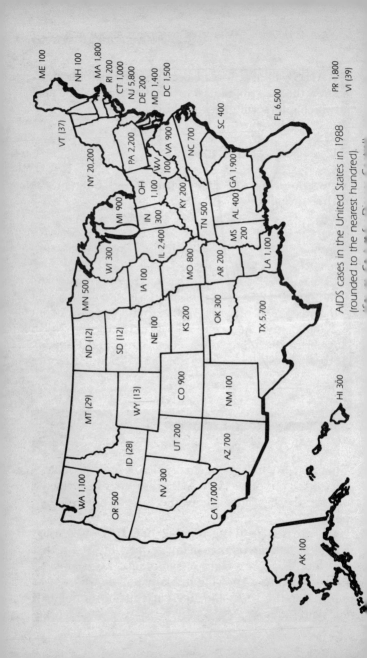

AIDS cases in the United States in 1988 (rounded to the nearest hundred).

ME 100
NH 100
MA 1,800
RI 200
CT 1,000
NJ 5,800
DE 200
MD 1,400
DC 1,500

VT [37]
NY 20,200
PA 2,200
WV 100
VA 900
NC 700
SC 400
FL 6,500

PR 1,800
VI (39)

MI 900
OH 1,100
IN 300
KY 200
TN 500
AL 400
GA 1,900
MS 200

WI 300
IL 2,400
IA 100
MO 800
AR 200
LA 1,100

MN 500
NE 100
KS 200
OK 300
TX 5,700

ND [12]
SD [12]

MT [29]
WY [13]
CO 900
NM 100

ID [28]
UT 200
AZ 700

WA 1,100
OR 500
NV 300
CA 17,000

HI 300

AK 100

AIDS will also spread because some people don't know the facts about how to avoid getting it. The next two chapters will give you these facts.

Questions and Answers

Question: Is the AIDS virus found only in the United States?

Answer: No. AIDS is an international epidemic, with at least 129 countries reporting AIDS cases. In January 1989 the World Health Organization estimated that about 377,000 people had become sick with AIDS worldwide. This is a very rough estimate, though, since some countries don't report many of the cases that appear. The estimate includes about 200,000 cases in Africa and 110,000 cases in North America (including the United States and Canada). About 40,000 cases have occurred in Latin America

Alon Reininger/Contact Press

and the Caribbean, 25,000 cases in Europe, 1,500 cases in Australia, New Zealand, and the Pacific, and about 500 cases in Asia.

Question: Can AIDS be spread by mosquitoes?
Answer: No. The virus doesn't spread through mosquitoes or any other insect bites because:

1. The amount of blood taken from a human by an insect is not sufficient to spread the AIDS virus.

2. When an insect bites a second human, it does not exchange blood.

3. The insect's digestive process alters the AIDS virus in such a way that it cannot spread to anyone.

4. If insect bites were a way of spreading the virus, there would be many more cases among older people and children where there are many mosquitoes. There aren't.

Question: Can I get the virus that causes AIDS by donating blood?
Answer: No. The equipment used to collect blood from donors in the United States, Canada, and Europe is disposable. There is no chance for the virus to get into a donor.

If you give blood, you can find out if you're already infected. Donated blood and blood products are tested for HIV. People who test positive are told of the results. But this is not a good way to get tested. (See Chapter 4.) If you know (or think) you might be infected with the virus that causes AIDS, then you should not donate blood. If you feel pressured to donate to a blood drive or to donate because a relative is

This is all you'll ever get from giving blood.

You won't get AIDS—The needles are sterile.*
So give blood and save lives.

* U.S. Public Health Service

in need, you can quietly tell the person taking the blood that you don't want it to be used. You can even call your local blood bank when you get home and explain that the blood you donated should not be used.

Question: Can people who get an organ transplant get AIDS?
Answer: Yes. However, this is very uncommon now. Donor organs (such as kidneys, hearts, and corneas) are all being tested for HIV.

Overheard in the gym . . .

Would you shake hands with somebody who has AIDS?

Sure I would. Didn't you hear what the school nurse said? Not through "casual contact." You don't get AIDS from gym towels, or doorknobs, or shaking hands—or passing somebody the ketchup, for Pete's sake!

Yeah, but what's that supposed to mean, "casual contact"? You can share a Coke—but no sloppy kissing? What's casual, and what's heavy duty? What if you got in the way of a sneeze?

Well, let's ask her! She said we could come in with any questions. . . .

From *Teens & AIDS: Playing It Safe* (© 1987, 1988 American Council of Life Insurance and Health Insurance Association of America)

Question: A boy in my class got the AIDS virus because he has hemophilia. What does that mean?

Answer: Hemophilia is an inherited blood disease that affects only males. People who have it do not have enough clotting factor in their blood. Without it, bruises, cuts, or internal bleeding can be dangerous, because the blood does not clot to stop the bleeding.

To correct this problem, they are given transfusions of this clotting factor. Each transfusion contains clotting factor gathered from as many as 5,000 different blood donations. Some hemophiliacs who received transfusions before May 1985, when blood screening began, got clotting factors that were infected with HIV. In fact, 7 or 8 out of every 10 hemophiliacs in some parts of America may have been infected with the AIDS virus. Some are only now beginning to show signs of HIV-related illnesses or AIDS.

All donated blood and blood products are now tested for HIV antibodies. In the United States it's very rare for the AIDS virus to be spread through transfusions.

Question: Does everyone who gets AIDS die?

Answer: We don't know. Three out of every 4 people with AIDS in America have died within three years of diagnosis. It will take more long-term studies to determine how long the others will live.

2

AIDS

AND

SEX

AIDS is a sexually transmitted disease. So the best way to avoid risking AIDS is to avoid sexual intercourse. Since many teens aren't having intercourse yet, they're safe—*for now*. But they still need the facts for when they do become sexually active—even if that's years in the future. Regardless of what you're doing (or not doing) now, as you read this chapter, remember that if your sexual partner has been exposed to the AIDS virus, he or she can give you AIDS. You should be concerned about your partner's past sexual activities, as well as your own present or future ones. So don't skip over certain sections just because you think, "*I'd* never do *that!*"

How the AIDS Virus Spreads Through Sexual Intercourse

Sex does not cause AIDS. Two people who do not have the AIDS virus can have sexual intercourse with each other for the rest of their lives and never get AIDS. But if HIV (the AIDS virus) is in a man's semen or a woman's vaginal fluids, sexual intercourse can pass HIV on.

HIV can enter a sex partner's body during *heterosexual vaginal intercourse* (when a man's penis enters a woman's vagina). When an infected man ejaculates (ejects semen into a woman's vagina), the HIV in his semen can infect the woman's body in several ways. It can enter her body through small ulcers, sores, or openings in the walls of the vagina. It can also infect the woman's immune cells, which are present in the vagina and in the vaginal fluids. It can also go directly into the cells that line the walls of the vagina. So HIV can infect a woman even when there are no sores or openings in her vagina.

Joanne Leonard/Woodfin Camp

An infected woman can also give the AIDS virus to a man. If HIV is in the cells or fluids in her vagina, it will come in contact with the skin of his penis during intercourse. The virus can enter his bloodstream the same way it enters a woman's: through sores or cuts, or by infecting the immune cells that are in his penis. HIV might also directly infect the cells in the urethra (the tube inside the penis that carries semen and urine).

HIV can also enter a sex partner's body during *anal intercourse* (when a man's penis enters the sex partner's rectum [anus]). Anal intercourse can involve two men or a man and a woman. When an infected man ejaculates, the HIV in his semen can pass into the cells of his partner's large intestine. HIV passes into the large intestine more easily than it does into the vagina and penis. The tissue that lines the large intestine is very thin and easily torn. So anal intercourse spreads HIV more easily than vaginal intercourse.

HIV may or may not be spread through *oral sex* (when a man's penis is placed in his partner's mouth, or when a woman's vaginal area is rubbed or stroked by her partner's mouth or tongue). In theory, infected semen or vaginal fluids might enter the sex partner's body through cells in the mouth, throat, or gums. So even women who have oral sex only with other women might be in danger of spreading the AIDS virus to each other. But compared with vaginal or anal intercourse, oral sex is much less likely to spread HIV.

Heterosexual Vaginal Intercourse

MAN TO WOMAN	WOMAN TO MAN
Infected man	Infected woman
↓	↓
has sexual intercourse with noninfected woman	has sexual intercourse with noninfected man
↓	↓
HIV in his semen goes into her white blood cells or the cells of her vagina	HIV in her vaginal cells or fluids goes into his white blood cells or the cells of his penis
↓	↓
Infected woman	Infected man

Safe-Sex Practices

Since AIDS is a sexually transmitted disease, abstinence (that is, no intercourse) is the only way to be 100 percent safe.

But couples who choose abstinence don't have to give up sexual pleasure. They can still enjoy other kinds of sexual activities where no body fluids are

Suddenly Sex Has Become Very Dangerous

exchanged. Activities that involve just the outside of both partners' bodies are completely safe. The following activities do not involve an exchange of body fluids and are considered safe.

Massage When massaging different parts of the body, many couples begin with a back rub. (A few drops of lotion, powder, or oil on the skin help the hands glide more easily over the body.) Then the partner giving the massage moves to the neck, the scalp, and the face. All parts of the body, even the toes, the knees, the ears, and the elbows, feel good when they're massaged.

Petting Couples can pet whether they are fully clothed or totally undressed. Either way, they can't get the AIDS virus by touching, pushing, and rubbing their bodies together. Nor will they get it by stroking their partner's vagina or penis, or by caressing their partner's chest, legs, buttocks, back, stomach, or arms. It's also safe to kiss or lick breasts or testicles. But be aware of the fact that some fluids can leak out of the

---

Since AIDS is a sexually transmitted disease, abstinence (that is, no intercourse) is the only way to be 100 percent safe. But couples who choose abstinence don't have to give up sexual pleasure.

penis *before* ejaculation. And a man might ejaculate during petting. So be sure the penis doesn't come in contact with the vagina. Even if the penis is not completely inside the vagina, fluids can still seep into the vaginal cells.

Masturbation   A person cannot get the AIDS virus if his or her body fluids do not have direct contact with anyone else's body fluids. So self-masturbation is perfectly safe.

Masturbating a sex partner is also safe. The AIDS virus cannot pass through unbroken skin. So people can get semen and vaginal fluids on their hands without worrying, unless they have open sores or cuts. In that case, they should wait until the cut or sore on the hand heals before touching their partner's body fluids.

Kissing   Couples can kiss each other anywhere on the outside of their bodies without getting or spreading the AIDS virus. Kissing on the lips is also safe. Deep tongue ("French") kissing *could* be risky. However, so far no cases of AIDS have been traced to deep tongue kissing. But very small amounts of HIV have been found in saliva. So HIV could possibly find its way into the body through cuts or sores in the mouth or gums. Until more is known, people with mouth sores, fever sores, swollen gums, or braces would be better off *not* deep tongue kissing.

Teenagers have always had to deal with the risks of an unplanned pregnancy and contracting sexually transmitted diseases. But the fear of contracting AIDS makes many who want to be sexually active feel angry and cheated. "It makes me kind of mad," says 18-year-

It isn't fair that sexual pleasure today is haunted by the nightmare of a deadly virus. But it's a reality.

old Dave. "I want to experiment, and to enjoy my sexuality. But instead I'm being choosy about who I date. I'm not going to risk getting AIDS by screwing around, but it just doesn't seem fair." Dave is right—it isn't fair that sexual pleasure today is haunted by the nightmare of a deadly virus. But it's a reality. It doesn't mean, however, that people can't enjoy their sexuality. Of the many ways they can express sexual feelings, only a few are risky.

Safer-Sex Guidelines

Those who choose to have sexual intercourse are risking exposure to HIV no matter what they do. There is no such thing as "safe" sexual intercourse anymore. But some sexual practices and behaviors are *safer* than others. The following "safer-sex" methods can reduce (but not eliminate) the chances of getting the AIDS virus.

There is no such thing as "safe" sexual intercourse anymore.

YOU CAN'T LIVE ON HOPE.

You hope this guy is finally the right guy.

You hope this time she just might be the one.

And you both hope the other one is not infected with the AIDS virus.

Of course you could ask. But your partner might not know. That's because it's possible to carry the AIDS virus for many years without showing any symptoms.

The only way to prevent getting infected is to protect yourself. Start using condoms. Every time.

AIDS Ask him to use them. If he says no, so can you.

If you think you can't get it, you're dead wrong.

Life preserver.

Wearing condoms saves lives. Maybe yours.
Your partner's. Or the lives of future partners.
  And though condoms can't cure AIDS, they can
stop it. But only if you wear them.
  So make a habit of sleeping with condoms.
As though your life depended on it.

Use condoms.
There's living proof they stop AIDS.

HERO

Health Education Resource Organization

945-AIDS • 251-1164 • 1-800-638-6252
Baltimore Metro   DC Metro   Elsewhere in MD

©1986. Created by Jeff McElhaney, Writer David Foote, Point Production Allan Saracher, Photography, for HERO.

USE A CONDOM

A condom (or rubber) is a soft, stretchable shield that is placed over the penis. It acts like a bag to collect the semen and keep it from entering the other person's body. It can be used during oral sex, as well as vaginal or anal intercourse. Condoms are commonly used to prevent pregnancy and sexually transmitted diseases. Now they also help control the spread of HIV by keeping semen from entering the sex partner's body. Condoms also keep the penis from touching vaginal or anal cells and fluids.

But condoms can't guarantee safety, because sometimes they break or slip off. Some condoms protect better than others.

Condoms made of latex are less likely to break or leak. They're better than "natural" or animal-skin condoms because they are consistently thick.

New condoms are stronger than old ones. As condoms age, the rubber they're made of becomes weaker. Heat is especially damaging, so wallets or glove compartments aren't good places to store them. The condom package has an expiration date on it, which tells when the condoms should no longer be used.

Even strong and reliable condoms can't protect you unless they're used right. Condoms are not reusable—a new one must be used each time a couple has sexual intercourse. Condoms go on before a couple *starts* sexual intercourse. If a man begins sexual intercourse, then withdraws to put on a condom, infected fluids could leak out of the penis even before ejaculation. And the penis could come into contact with infected vaginal fluids.

Condoms have to be put on correctly. They come rolled up into a ring, which should be rolled directly

Even strong and reliable condoms can't protect you unless they're used right.

onto an *erect* penis. It shouldn't be put on a limp penis, or be unrolled and then stretched over the penis. Some condoms have a special tip at the end to collect semen. If a condom doesn't have this tip, about one-half inch of room should be left between the tip of the penis and the tip of the condom. That space is needed to collect the semen.

Condoms also have to be taken off right. After ejaculation, the penis becomes smaller. The condom could slip off and spill semen. When the man withdraws his penis from his partner, he should *hold on to the condom*. When his penis is completely out, he should take the condom off and throw it away. It's a good idea for him to wash his hands and penis before going back to his partner. If intercourse is repeated, a new condom must be used.

A spermicidal cream can give extra protection. It (or a contraceptive water-based jelly or foam) is put into the tip of the condom before the condom goes on. Chemicals like nonoxynol-9 may help stop HIV, as well as sperm. But petroleum jelly and other lubricants that aren't water-based don't stop the virus, and they can damage the condom. So they should never be used with a condom.

No one needs a prescription to buy condoms. Drug stores sell them with other birth-control items, like contraceptive creams and jellies and spermicides. Sometimes they're kept behind the counter. If you

The right way to use a condom.

1. Place the rolled-up condom on the end of the erect penis. Hold the tip of the condom (about a half-inch) to squeeze out the air. This leaves room for the semen to collect after ejaculation.

2. Keep holding the tip of the condom with one hand. With the other hand, unroll the condom down the length of the erect penis. (Uncircumcised men should first pull back the foreskin.)

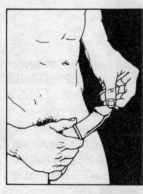

3. Unroll the condom all the way down to the pubic hair.

4. Put the condom on before entering your partner.

5. You can use a water-based lubricant (check the label or ask a pharmacist) such as K-Y Lubricating Jelly or Today Personal Lubricant. Oil-based lubricants like mineral oil, baby oil, vegetable oil, petroleum jelly, cold cream, or vaseline should *not* be used, since they can damage the condom.

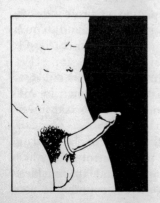

6. Right after ejaculation: (a) hold onto the condom as you (b) pull out while the penis is still erect.

don't see them—ask! Condoms are even sold in some vending machines in rest rooms, locker rooms, hotel lobbies, and on some college campuses.

Now that you know the *facts*, here are some hard questions:

→ Who's responsible for making sure condoms are used—the man or the woman?

→ How do you tell your partner that you want to use condoms?

→ What if your partner refuses to use condoms?

Here are *our* answers:

1. Who's responsible for making sure condoms are used during sexual intercourse? *You* are. Whether you're male or female doesn't matter. You have to take care of yourself. If you haven't been exposed to HIV, you should use condoms to stay that way. If you have been exposed to HIV (or suspect you might have been), you should use condoms to protect your partner. Most HIV-positive people have no symptoms, so your partner wouldn't suspect that you have it. If your partner contracts HIV from you, he or she could unknowingly pass it on to someone else, and so on. It would be up to you to prevent this chain reaction by using a condom.

Even if you're already infected, a condom could still protect you. An immune system weakened by HIV will have trouble fighting other sexually transmitted diseases like syphilis, gonorrhea, or herpes. These diseases could also trigger the onset of HIV-related symptoms. If an infected person's immune system isn't burdened by other illnesses, it might be able to fight off AIDS symptoms for a longer period of time.

Most people prefer to use latex condoms that come prelubri-
cated. Many people also like to supply additional lubricant.
Using the right lubricants can lessen the chances of a condom
breaking. Water-based lubricants like those pictured above are
safe to use with a latex condom. . . .

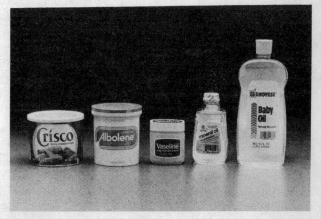

. . . But the wrong lubricants can greatly increase the risk of
breakage. Oil-based lubricants like those pictured above
weaken latex considerably and are *not* safe to use with a
condom.

Don't die of embarrassment.

Yes, it could be embarrassing to ask a man to wear a condom, especially if you don't know him very well.

But that's exactly who you need to ask—the man you don't know.

And if he says no, so can you.

Because you just can't be sure who's infected with the AIDS virus.

Not having sex is one sure way to avoid AIDS. If you decide to have sex, using a condom is your best protection.

It's as simple as that.

AIDS is incurable, and if you get it, you'll likely die.

So start carrying condoms and tell your partner to use them.

Because the consequences of getting AIDS are more than

AIDS just a little embarrassing. They're deadly.

If you think you can't get it, you're dead wrong.

NEW YORK CITY DEPARTMENT OF HEALTH. FOR MORE INFORMATION CALL: **1 (718) 485-8111**

Mary carries condoms in her purse at all times. During National Condom Week she told a reporter, "A year ago I wouldn't be caught dead with a condom, but now it's like a credit card—you don't leave home without it." Like Mary, anyone planning to have intercourse should always have a supply of condoms.

"A year ago I wouldn't be caught dead with a condom, but now it's like a credit card—you don't leave home without it."

---

2. How do you tell your partner you want to use condoms? It's easiest to bring up the subject of condoms early, before a sexual relationship starts. You don't have to start out by talking about the two of you using them. Instead, talk about the general topic of AIDS and condoms. For example, tell your date about the billboard advertisements shown on pages 50–51. Or tell him or her about the AIDS education group at Dartmouth College that sponsors condom races: The participants hold a broomstick between their legs and race to see who can put a condom on the stick the fastest. Discuss how condoms have become a fact of sex. (They can even look romantic: condom bouquets are now being sold by some florists, and many condoms are now available in fancy colors such as pink, purple, green, and yellow.)

Many people know they should use condoms during sexual intercourse, and want to use them. But often they find it embarrassing to bring up the subject. Very often *both* partners want to use condoms, but each is afraid to tell the other. It's easier if you realize that your partner will probably be happy and relieved at your suggestion. If it's hard to bring up the subject face-to-face, try writing a letter or talking on the phone. But don't leave it till the last minute, when you're in the middle of sex. It's difficult to break off a

passionate kiss to ask, "Do you want to use a condom?" Make it easier on yourself by planning ahead.

Robin is in love with Tom. He's fun to be with, he's sensitive, romantic, handsome, and loving. He is everything Robin ever wanted in a boyfriend. But he used to shoot drugs, so Robin is worried that he may be infected with HIV. At first she wasn't concerned; all she wanted was Tom. He used IV drugs only a short time. He looked very healthy. And she was afraid to risk losing him by asking whether he planned to wear a condom if they had intercourse. But then Robin thought of a plan that would protect her *and* show Tom she loved him. One night she asked Tom to take her out for Chinese food. After they ate, she gave him a fortune cookie with a condom rolled up inside. "Want me to tell you your fortune?" she asked him with a shy smile. "You're going to make love to a beautiful girl who loves you very much and wants to be close to you tonight. She wants you to have this and enjoy yourself." Tom slipped the con-

dom into his pocket, took Robin's hand, and led her out of the restaurant. With one fortune cookie and a condom, Robin had told Tom that they could take care of both birth control and AIDS prevention together.

There are some people who will agree that using a condom is important for everyone else in the world, but not for them. What if your partner says, "Don't you trust me? Don't you love me?" When Jim faced this problem, he took Kelly for a walk so they could talk in private. He wanted her to understand that it was because he loved her so much that a condom was important. "I don't want anything to ruin what we have," he told her. "If I use a condom, it's an added prevention against pregnancy. And it will protect both of us from any sexually transmitted disease. Some diseases don't even have symptoms. What if I got one from somebody else before I met you, and I don't even know it yet? I couldn't stand it if I passed it on to you. I'll be able to enjoy our time together more if I'm not so worried about pregnancy and diseases. I love you, Kelly," Jim said, "but I need to love you in a way that makes me comfortable. Okay?" Jim knew it was "okay" when Kelly wrapped her arms around him and held him close.

Jim Anderson/Woodfin Camp

3. What if your partner refuses to use condoms? You face a very difficult decision. Should you protect yourself from HIV but risk losing your partner? Or should you continue the relationship but risk exposure to the AIDS virus? The logical answer is that you should protect yourself. But the loss of someone who means a lot to you can cause strong emotional pain. Fear of such pain may keep you from acting logically.

Before you decide, take some time to calculate your chance of getting HIV through sexual intercourse. That chance depends on four things: (1) how common HIV is in the group of people your partner has had sexual intercourse with; (2) the number of contacts your partner has had; (3) the kind of intercourse you're having, since each has a different degree of risk (oral sex, for example, is less risky than vaginal intercourse, and anal intercourse is by far the most risky); and (4) whether or not you're using a condom.

If you have vaginal intercourse with an infected person once, your chances of becoming infected are at least 10 times greater if you don't use a condom than if you do use one. But your risk of infection goes up with the number of times you have sex. If you have vaginal intercourse with an infected partner many times, even if you use a condom every time your chance of becoming infected is about 1 in 11, since condoms may break, tear, or spill. But if you don't use a condom, your chances of becoming infected go way up to 2 out of 3.

It's clearly much more dangerous to have unprotected sex with someone who has practiced high-risk behavior than with someone who hasn't. But the fact remains: You simply can't tell what people have done in their past by looking at them, so protecting yourself is the best thing you can do.

Try to find out *why* your partner won't use condoms before you break off the relationship. Often a refusal is a cover-up for some fear or worry. People who haven't tried condoms may have worries like these:

FELICIA: "When I make love, it's a very romantic and passionate act. I don't want my lover to break the mood to put on a condom."

KAZUO: "My friends say that if I use a condom, sex won't feel as good."

DAVE: "Condoms are a real turnoff. I'd probably lose my erection if I stopped to put one on."

Despite these fears, condoms can be used with great ease and comfort and without affecting either your performance or the romantic mood. But it takes some practice. If you're a boy and you're shy about using condoms, buy a package and practice putting them on. In no time you'll be able to slip one on with ease and certainly without losing your erection. If you're a girl, buy a package and look at one closely to see what it's like and how it feels. Practice by putting one on a medium-size cucumber, a banana, or a zucchini. You might also try helping your boyfriend use them. Some

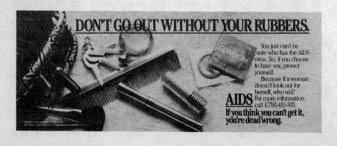

Condoms can be used with great ease and comfort and without affecting either your performance or the romantic mood.

---

couples find that practice sessions help them overcome any initial awkwardness and can also be a lot of fun.

BE MONOGAMOUS

To be monogamous (muh-NAH-guh-muss) means to have a long-term relationship with only *one* sex partner. If neither you nor your steady lover has used intravenous drugs, had sexual intercourse with high-risk partners (IV drug users, male homosexuals, or bisexuals), or had blood or blood-product transfusions before May 1985, then neither of you is likely to be infected with HIV. If you have intercourse only with each other, you don't have to worry about getting the AIDS virus.

The only risk that people in monogamous, drug-free relationships have is the possibility that previous sex partners were infected. If your boyfriend had sex with another male two years ago, are you absolutely sure he'd tell you? If your girlfriend had a few sex partners while away on vacation last year, how would you know about it? Or if your partner injected drugs when he or she went out with other friends, would you know? The fact is, it's often difficult to be sure about a person's past. Your partner could have the virus and not even know it. Because HIV can stay in the body for many years without causing any signs or symptoms, many people think they're being honest when they say they don't have the AIDS virus because they don't have AIDS. But even when a person has no symptoms, that person's virus can still spread to his or her partner. Because of these problems, having only one partner in a long-term relationship doesn't guarantee protection from HIV infection. But together with condom use, it makes sexual intercourse a much safer activity than unprotected, unlimited sex.

LIMIT THE NUMBER OF SEXUAL PARTNERS

HIV can spread during sexual intercourse. So the more people you have intercourse with, the greater the chance that one of your partners is infected.

Sixteen-year-old Karen knows she could get the AIDS virus by having many sexual relationships. But even though she has many sex partners, she doesn't think she has to worry. "I've grown up with the guys I have sex with," said Karen. "I know they're not bisexuals or drug addicts. I protect myself by having intercourse only with people I know." But Karen isn't as well protected as she thinks. If somewhere along the line one of Karen's partners had intercourse with an HIV-infected person, he may have become infected. When he has sex with Karen, he could pass it along to her. Karen's friends would not intentionally spread the AIDS virus to her. But most infected teenagers have no symptoms, so the AIDS virus can be spread unknowingly.

Today, during the AIDS epidemic, only abstinence can keep you totally safe from contracting HIV through sexual intercourse. But if abstinence isn't a

PROCEED
WITH
CONDOMS

The more sexual partners
you have, the greater your
risk of contracting AIDS.
Use condoms and limit
your sexual partners.

realistic choice for you, then remember these safer-sex guidelines:

→ Use a condom.

→ Be monogamous.

→ If you can't be monogamous, limit the number of sexual partners.

Your sexuality is a natural expression of yourself. It gives you a way to feel good about yourself and about others. But if you don't protect yourself from the virus that causes AIDS, it can also be dangerous. When you use the safe-sex practices and safer-sex guidelines described in this chapter, you can be emotionally and physically close to another person without worrying about HIV.

Questions and Answers

Question: Can a spermicidal cream or jelly alone protect a girl from getting AIDS?
Answer: No. The ingredient in spermicides called nonoxynol-9 acts as a *chemical* barrier. But it should be used with a *physical* barrier—a condom. Even then, *neither totally eliminates the risk of infection*, since a con-

---

The more people you have intercourse with, the greater the chance that one of your partners is infected.

Alon Reininger/Contact Press

Salsa musician and film actor Ruben Blades, with a condom package.

dom can break. A contraceptive sponge that contains nonoxynol-9 can help keep HIV from spreading, but it hasn't been proven totally effective. A condom is the only birth-control device that can be used for both birth control and AIDS prevention. Other birth-control devices, like the Pill (oral contraceptives) or diaphragm, will not protect you from the AIDS virus.

Question: Can I get HIV by sitting on the toilet in a public bathroom?
Answer: No. The virus doesn't last once it is exposed to air outside the body, blood, or other tissues containing the virus. It is also easily killed by detergents, disinfectants, and bleach.

Question: Will douching after sexual intercourse help wash out semen that's infected with HIV?
Answer: No. The AIDS virus infects cells in the vagina immediately upon contact. There is no time to try to flush it out with douching.

Question: I read that I don't really have to worry about getting HIV through heterosexual intercourse. Is that true?
Answer: No. Only 4 out of every 100 reported *adult* AIDS cases are linked with heterosexual intercourse. But twice that many (8 out of every 100) of the reported AIDS cases among *adolescents* are linked to heterosexual intercourse. With teenage girls alone, roughly one-half of all AIDS cases are linked to heterosexual intercourse.

Second, the number of actual AIDS cases spread through heterosexual intercourse may be higher than statistics show. Some of the people counted in the IV-

Esther Brumberg

drug-user group may actually have gotten the virus by sexual intercourse. Also, people who are newly infected won't be counted as AIDS cases until they become sick. That can take many years. (The average is now thought to be eight years, but it may be as long as fifteen years.) So the number of cases may be much higher as time passes.

Question: My boyfriend and I have been having unprotected sex for six months. Is there any reason he should start using a condom now?
Answer: Yes. If your boyfriend is infected, he may already have passed the virus on to you. But there is also a possibility that you are still uninfected.

Compare it to the risk of getting pregnant. Just because you don't get pregnant the first few months you have unprotected sex doesn't mean you won't ever get pregnant. Your chances of getting pregnant increase every time you have unprotected sex. The same is true about the AIDS virus. It's never too late to protect yourself.

If you know your sex partner shares IV drug needles, has unprotected intercourse, or has intercourse with people who do, you should think about being tested for the virus. Talk with a counselor who can advise you on this. (See Chapter 4 for details on testing.)

Question: If I have questions about homosexuality, or if I think or know that I am gay and want information, what should I do?
Answer: To get the information you need:

1. Call a gay hotline in your community or in a nearby city. The number is probably in your phone book.

Overheard in the classroom . . .

Come on, Mr. Harris—how could you ask somebody you just met: "Are you healthy?"

What are you supposed to do, take an AIDS test on your first date?

Rubbers? I'd be embarrassed to carry them in my purse.

Hey, hey, keep the volume down!

Every home room is having a session on AIDS, so let's go. First, AIDS isn't going to jump from behind a tree and get you! It doesn't just happen. If you get involved with unsafe sex or needle drugs, you put yourself in danger. But you *can* be safe—if you put some limits on what you do.

I suppose what I'm trying to say is: *Let's be careful out there.* These days, anybody who thinks love should be blind hasn't heard about AIDS. Love needs to be *smart,* starting here and now. Real life isn't something that starts when you turn 18 or 21. You're making decisions right now that could hurt you—or save your life.

From *Teens & AIDS: Playing It Safe* (© 1987, 1988 American Council of Life Insurance and Health Insurance Association of America)

2. Contact a nearby college to ask if there is a gay group or organization you can get in touch with.

3. Contact one of the national organizations, like the Hetrick-Martin Institute in New York City, listed in the "Call for Help" resource section at the back of this book.

3

AIDS

AND

DRUGS

How the AIDS Virus Spreads Through Intravenous Drug Use

SHARING NEEDLES AND SYRINGES WITH INFECTED DRUG USERS

The most direct connection between the AIDS virus and drugs is the needle and syringe. If either is contaminated with HIV, the drug user can be infected. Whether the needle is used for intravenous (IV) drug use (shooting drugs directly into a vein) or for "skin-popping" (injecting drugs under the skin), both methods can spread HIV.

The needle is connected to a hollow tube called a syringe, which holds the drug. The needle and syringe together are sometimes called the "works" or a "set." When a user shoots up, the drug is injected through the syringe and needle into the user's skin, muscle, or bloodstream. A small amount of blood or tissue juice always flows backward into the needle and syringe top. If the set is used again by another person, that blood or tissue juice mixes with the drug and is then injected into the next user's veins or skin. Therefore, if infected users share their sets with other users, their infected blood or tissue juice may be in the syringe—and may be injected into the next user.

Sixteen-year-old Keith got HIV through IV drug use. He knew the danger of sharing needles. He avoided places called shooting galleries, where needles are passed around. But sometimes sharing a needle was the only way Keith could use drugs. "It's easy to say 'Don't share needles,'" he said. "But it's not that simple, because needles aren't easy to get. I can't always carry one around with me, and I sure don't

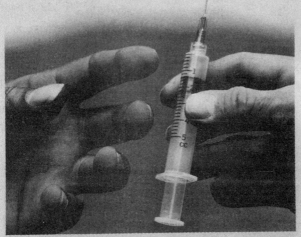

SHARING NEEDLES CAN GET YOU MORE THAN HIGH.

IT CAN GET YOU AIDS.

You can't tell if someone has the AIDS virus just by looking.

You can't tell if needles or works are infected just by looking.

When you shoot drugs and share needles or works you could get AIDS. Even if you think your drug-sharing partners are clean, if the AIDS virus is present, it could be passed to you.

AIDS is not pretty. It's a long, slow, painful way to die. Do the right thing. Get into treatment. It's the best way to make sure you don't shoot up AIDS.

STOP SHOOTING UP AIDS.
GET INTO DRUG TREATMENT
CALL 1-800 662 HELP.

A Public Service of the National Institute on Drug Abuse, Department of Health and Human Services.

Wide World

keep one at home—I don't want my parents or little brother to find it. So sometimes I have to use a friend's needle. I thought I was being careful. Most of the time I held the used needle over a match because I thought that would clean it. Now I know it doesn't. I knew IV drug use could spread AIDS, but I never thought it would happen to me."

There are approximately 1.2 million IV-drug-using addicts in this country. Among them are 25 of every 100 people who have AIDS. Unfortunately, these numbers are likely to continue rising. Each year thousands of drug addicts who want help are not able to enter drug rehabilitation programs, which are either too expensive or overcrowded or not available at all. Only 12 percent of America's drug users who are actively seeking help are now receiving it. Teenagers face additional obstacles, because in most states methadone maintenance treatment is given only to people over 18. So even when drug users want to stop, many can't get the help they need.

In 1988 the Presidential Commission on the HIV Epidemic pointed out that the threat of AIDS tomorrow doesn't stop an addict's need for drugs today. The people on the panel insisted that, to slow the spread of AIDS in the United States, more attention and money should be given to the problem of intravenous drug use. They proposed opening 3,300 new drug treatment centers that would provide new treatment slots for 400,000 to 500,000 drug users. Many consider this approach more realistic than blaming the drug user and turning away from the problem.

The transfer of infected blood through intravenous drug use is what spreads the AIDS virus—not the drug itself. You cannot get HIV from drugs that are smoked (like marijuana or cocaine); swallowed (like

---

The threat of AIDS tomorrow doesn't stop an addict's need for drugs today.

---

uppers, downers, or alcohol); or snorted (like cocaine). But if you get high or drunk, you may forget about the dangers of unprotected sex or sharing a needle.

Lisa, for example, insisted that she could not have the AIDS virus because, although her boyfriend was an IV drug user, they had been careful to practice only safer sex. But when she discussed her infection with an AIDS counselor, she remembered that there were a few times when she had had too much to drink and had then had unprotected sex.

The use of crack (a non-intravenous drug derived from cocaine) is also linked with exposure to HIV. Crack is alarmingly addictive. Many crack users have become addicted after trying it only a few times. Once teenagers are addicted to crack (or cocaine or heroin), they often use sex as a way either to obtain the drug or to obtain money to buy the drug. This puts them at double risk: Having many sexual partners increases the risk of HIV exposure; and the people these teens have sexual intercourse with are often HIV carriers.

HAVING SEXUAL INTERCOURSE
WITH INFECTED DRUG USERS

Eighteen-year-old Ginny believes she got HIV by having sexual intercourse with her infected boyfriend. Ginny planned to join the army after high school. As part of the military recruit health-screening program, she was tested for HIV. Ginny was shocked when she was told that the test result was positive. "I know I didn't get it from shooting drugs or having anal intercourse, because I never did those things," she said. "So I think I must have gotten it from having sex with my boyfriend. I can't prove it, because he's never been

tested. But he used to shoot drugs, and I'll bet he has the AIDS virus."

At this point Ginny doesn't know what she'll do. Because of her positive test results, the army won't take her. Her boyfriend left her when she accused him of giving her the AIDS virus. She knows that if she has a child, there's a 30 to 65 percent chance that the baby will get the virus. She's also worried about passing the virus to other men. She knows that once people are infected, they risk spreading the disease every time they have sexual intercourse.

Ginny knew her boyfriend was an IV drug user, and she knew IV drug use spreads the AIDS virus. But because he had no symptoms of the disease, she thought she was safe. If Ginny could go back in time, she certainly would use safer-sex practices. But for her there's no second chance. Now she spends many of her days at home, depressed, lonely, and worried about dying after a long and painful illness.

BABIES BORN TO INFECTED IV DRUG USERS

Carla was an IV drug user for six months when she was 16. Then at age 19 she became pregnant. The doctor wanted her to have a blood test to check for HIV, but Carla didn't want to do it. "I felt fine," she said. "I had no symptoms. I'd only tried drugs for a short time three years ago when things were messed up in my life, but then I stopped. I graduated from high school, and I have a job. I never thought AIDS could happen to me or my baby. Now that I know the facts, it's too late." Carla's baby was born carrying the AIDS virus.

By the end of 1988, over 1,100 babies had been born with the AIDS virus. Nearly 8 out of every 10 babies

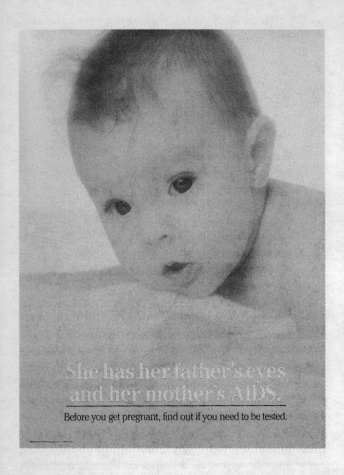

She has her father's eyes
and her mother's AIDS.

Before you get pregnant, find out if you need to be tested.

born with HIV were from families where at least one parent was an IV drug user. In New York City, where HIV is present in well over half of all IV drug users, 1 in every 61 babies is born with HIV antibodies.

Not all babies born with HIV antibodies will actually be infected with the AIDS virus. The baby's blood may contain only the HIV antibodies—and not the HIV—passed on from the infected mother. In that case, the baby will lose the HIV antibodies in six to eighteen months. But 30 to 65 percent of the babies born with HIV antibodies actually do have the virus and will develop AIDS. Seventy-five percent of them will die before the age of two.

Prevention of AIDS

If you don't inject drugs into your body, you'll never have to worry about injecting the AIDS virus. But even if you avoid IV drugs, you can still get the AIDS virus by having sexual intercourse with an infected IV drug user. You can protect yourself from this route of transmission by abstaining from sex, or by using the safer-sex practices described in Chapter 2.

AIDS prevention also relies on the message you give to your friends. If you don't use drugs, tell your friends. Let them know why you've made this decision. If you do use drugs, don't push it on your friends. Let them know that if they decide against drugs, it's okay with you. If friends share IV drug needles, tell them how it can spread the AIDS virus. By talking to your friends about AIDS and IV drug use, you may save a life.

If you don't inject drugs into your body, you'll never have to worry about injecting the AIDS virus.

I wish I never did it. I wish I could take it back. Every night,

I go to bed praying that I'll wake up back in time. That never happens.

I didn't want a baby yet. I didn't want AIDS. I didn't want a baby with AIDS.

Don't ask for AIDS. DON'T GET IT.

If you already use intravenous drugs, the best way to avoid HIV infection is to stop. This may not be easy, but give it some thought. Think about why you started. Are those reasons still valid? Are drugs solving problems for you, or adding to your problems? Think about the ways drugs are hurting you or your family. You know that drugs are bad for you and your health and that using them is against the law. You know that they're expensive and that you could die from an overdose. And now you know that they put you at risk of getting HIV. Take a good look at your life. That can be the first step in getting drugs out of your life.

Get the facts you need to make this decision. See "Call for Help" at the back of this book. It lists the names and numbers of drug rehabilitation centers that can help you. The people at these centers can answer most or all of your questions. They know where you can get outpatient (that is, without overnight stay) help and counseling with or without your parents' knowledge. Or they can help you decide what to do about your parents or family. Sometimes you can make changes more easily by changing where you live for a while. You may have a better chance of starting a new life after spending some time in a hospital or after joining a residential treatment program. It takes time, help, and knowledge to change a drug habit. You can get a good start by reading through the "Call for Help" section.

If you decide you can't (or won't) stop shooting drugs right now, here's how to keep yourself as safe as possible:

→ *Never* share your needle and syringe with anyone.

→ *Always* clean your set before and after each use. Fill the syringe with bleach, then flush the bleach through the needle into a sink, toilet, or container. Do the same thing again. Then fill the syringe with

Take a good look at your life. That can be the first step in getting drugs out of your life.

1. **Bleach**

2. **Water**

(a) Fill syringe | (b) Empty syringe | (a) Fill syringe | (b) Empty syringe

(c) Fill syringe | (d) Empty syringe | (c) Fill syringe | (d) Empty syringe

Make sure you don't shoot or drink the bleach.

How to clean used needles and syringes. If you use someone else's "set," clean it with bleach, then water—but don't shoot or drink the bleach! Bleach kills the AIDS virus, which gets into used needles and syringes. By cleaning with bleach, you will help protect yourself from getting AIDS, and bleach will not damage the needle.

clean water (it's best to boil the water first), and flush the water through the needle into a sink, toilet, or container. Repeat the procedure with clean water.

→ Avoid cleaning methods that don't work, like boiling your set in water for a minute or holding it over a lighted match.

→ Don't buy your set on the street. Many street sellers have needles they say are new, but they're really used. If the law in your state prohibits the sale of hypodermic needles without a prescription, you can call your local department of health and ask if your city offers a "clean needle" program for drug users. Some city officials are hoping to slow the spread of AIDS by exchanging new IV needles for used ones. This approach has helped decrease the spread of HIV among IV drug users in Scotland, Wales, and other European countries. If you do buy a needle on the street, clean it with bleach, as described above, before using it.

If you have already shared needles or had sex with an infected IV drug user, you may be infected with the AIDS virus. The next chapter will discuss when, how, why, and where to get tested.

Questions and Answers

Question: Could I have gotten the HIV infection that causes AIDS from the needle that was used to pierce my ears?

Answer: The answer is "Yes" if that same needle was already used by other people. They may have left

At Boston City Hospital, a superhero character called Bleachman, from the San Francisco AIDS Foundation, shows how the use of bleach can help clean shared IV drug needles and syringes.

infected blood on the needle. But the amount of infected blood that could be on the tip of an ear-piercing needle is very small compared to the large amount in a set used by a drug user. There is no documented case of this happening.

The answer is "No" if you got your ears pierced at a place like a department store, a clinic, or a doctor's office that uses a brand-new needle and post for each person.

Question: My friend says that I could get AIDS by getting a tattoo. Is that true?
Answer: Yes. As with ear-piercing, you could get the AIDS virus if the tattooing needle was already used on a person who has HIV. The answer is "No" if you get your tattoo at a place that uses new needles for every customer. But there's a better chance of getting the AIDS virus from a tattooing needle than from an ear-piercing needle. In tattooing, the dye needles must be injected into your skin many times, so there are many more chances for the AIDS virus to get into your body. A tattooing needle is also more likely to be contaminated, because IV drug users often get tattoos to cover up their track marks (scars left by the needles).

Question: I use a needle and syringe to inject body-building hormones. Can I get AIDS from doing this?
Answer: As with ear-piercing and tattooing, you risk getting AIDS only when you share your needle and syringe with an infected person. But keep in mind that using bodybuilding androgens has been linked with a lot of other very serious health problems, including high blood pressure and sterility.

Overheard on the bus . . .

Me, I think I'll pass on drugs—and wait on sex.

Mr. Harris really makes you think, that's for sure. It's hard to figure, though. He says people who sleep around have a bigger chance of getting AIDS. He says if you don't have sex and don't shoot up, you're pretty safe. But what if somebody *used* to go with somebody who did drugs? What if somebody's worried about *already* being sick?

Mr. Harris said there was a test, remember? And a clinic downtown that gives it—no questions asked.

Yeah, and there's that hotline to call too. . . .

From *Teens & AIDS: Playing It Safe* (© 1987, 1988 American Council of Life Insurance and Health Insurance Association of America)

Question: Can I get AIDS from a marijuana cigarette that gets passed around to a lot of people?
Answer: No. This is a form of casual contact. But getting high can certainly affect your judgment and make you take chances with sex and drugs that can put you at risk.

Question: Can I get AIDS from the needle they use when I donate blood?
Answer: No. Blood donors in the United States have their blood drawn with new sterilized needles and tubes that are disposed of after one use.

Question: I'm not addicted to drugs, but sometimes I do use a needle to inject drugs. Can I get HIV even though I'm not a drug addict?
Answer: Yes. Anyone who has shared IV needles and syringes at any time since the late 1970s could be infected with the AIDS virus.

TESTING

The Tests

Three kinds of tests can now be given to people who want to know if they've been infected with HIV. Researchers use these tests to follow the course of AIDS in a given person, to learn how the virus spreads and changes over time, and to learn about the effectiveness of various treatments. Researchers also use the results of these tests to follow the course of the AIDS epidemic.

ANTIBODY TESTS

When a person is infected with the AIDS virus, the immune system produces antibodies, which move through the blood. The most common tests for the AIDS virus are blood tests that look for these antibodies. If they are found, the person is most likely infected with HIV.

There are two kinds of antibody tests: (1) The *ELISA* (*e*nzyme-*l*inked *i*mmun*o*sorbent *a*ssay) test detects antibodies manufactured when the body is infected by HIV. (2) The *Western blot* test is used to double-check blood samples that the *ELISA* test shows to be positive. It also detects HIV antibodies, but it's a more specific test and is more difficult and more expensive to perform.

These HIV-antibody tests were first used in May 1985 as a way of checking donated blood for HIV infection. Before the blood supply was screened, about 12,000 Americans were infected with HIV from blood transfusions. But now the risk of infection from blood transfusion is 1 in 40,000. This is much less than your chances of dying from the flu (1 in 5,000) or of dying in a car accident (1 in 5,000 per year).

Lynne Weinstein/Woodfin Camp

ANTIGEN TESTS

Antigen (AN-tih-juhn) tests detect the HIV itself, rather than its antibodies. An antigen causes the body to produce antibodies. The word comes from *anti-body gen*erator. Different kinds of antigen tests detect different parts of the virus: the whole virus, the outer coat, the inner core, or special proteins made by the virus. Antigen tests used along with antibody tests can tell whether a person is infected, as well as what stage of infection the person is in.

VIRAL CULTURES

A viral culture is a laboratory test in which medical workers grow HIV from the cells or body fluids of an infected person. Even when a person is definitely in-fected, however, the virus may not always grow. So cultures are used only in combination with other types of tests.

Getting the Test

Getting the test for HIV is a fairly simple process. But making the decision to have the test is more complicated. Before blood is taken, a counselor should explain the advantages and disadvantages of HIV testing (see pages 99–100). Then you should ask questions (see pages 103–104). It takes some time to understand fully the impact that an HIV test can have on your life, as we will discuss later in this chapter. So it may be best for you to leave after the counseling session, and then return for the test only after you've had a chance to think it over.

If you decide to have the test after this counseling, then a doctor, nurse, or technician will draw some blood from your arm. To do this, a rubber strap or tube is wrapped around your upper arm. Alcohol is used to clean the skin in the bend of the elbow or near a vein in your hand or arm. A needle with a syringe attached is inserted into a vein, and blood is drawn. (A new disposable needle and syringe are used for each person, so there is no chance of getting HIV during the testing procedure.) It takes just a few seconds to draw the needed blood (about enough to fill a teaspoon). Although you'll feel a sharp jab when the needle is inserted, drawing blood is not a very painful

---

Getting the test for HIV is a fairly simple process. But making the decision to have the test is more complicated.

procedure. The rubber strap is unwrapped, and a piece of cotton or gauze is pressed against the skin to prevent any bleeding. The blood is put into a small test tube. The needle and syringe are thrown away.

This blood sample is sent to a testing laboratory. There the blood is given the ELISA test. If it is positive, the blood is retested with the Western blot, to make certain. Sometimes an antigen test that looks directly for the virus is also done. Because so many people are having these tests, the labs have a great deal of work to do, so it will probably be a few weeks before you know the results.

How you are told the results depends on where you are tested. Few, if any, testing sites have a policy of sending the results to you in a letter. Most ask you to come in for a personal talk.

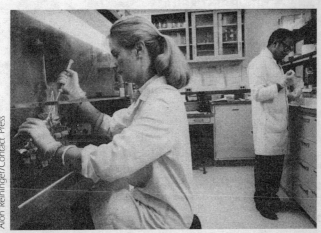

AIDS research being done at New York's St. Luke's—Roosevelt Hospital.

Alon Reininger/Contact Press

Limitations of the Test

NOT A TEST FOR AIDS

A positive test result does *not* mean that the person has AIDS. It means that he or she has probably been *infected with* HIV—the virus that causes AIDS. Some experts think that about 1 out of every 3 people with a positive HIV test will get an AIDS-related disease within five years of being infected. Others think that *everyone* who has HIV will develop AIDS eventually. Right now no test can predict for sure. Researchers have been studying AIDS for such a short time that they can't say whether a person can stay healthy after being infected with HIV. But the longer a person has HIV, the more likely he or she is to get sick and die.

FALSE-POSITIVE TEST RESULTS

Sometimes the test result may be positive when, in fact, the tested person does *not* have HIV. This "false-positive" result is most likely to happen with a person who does *not* do the things that spread HIV—people who have never used IV drugs, had transfusions, or had sexual intercourse with IV drug users, male bisexuals, or homosexuals. Only 1 in about 10,000 of these low-risk people will be infected. The chance of an uninfected person getting a false-positive result is also about 1 in 10,000. So, if 1 million low-risk people were tested, 200 would be found to be positive by ELISA plus Western blot tests. But only 100 would actually be infected. The other 100 would have false-positive tests and would not actually be infected.

HIV testing is much more accurate for people who have a reason to suspect that they might be positive.

When people who engage in high-risk behavior (see page 96) are tested, the HIV antibody and antigen tests are almost always accurate. More than 99 times out of 100, a positive test result means that a person really is infected with HIV.

FALSE-NEGATIVE TEST RESULTS

Sometimes HIV tests may turn out negative when the person really is infected with HIV. This "false-negative" result can occur during the "window period." That is the time it takes (usually from a few weeks to six months) for the body to produce enough antibodies to be detected by the tests. If a person is tested shortly after being infected, the body may not yet have made enough antibodies or antigens to give the correct test result. The test result could be negative even though the infection is really there.

A negative result is usually correct if, in the six months before taking the blood test, you have not shared IV drug needles or had sexual intercourse with a potentially infected person. (Some people infected with HIV may not develop antibodies for a year or more. But this is true of only a very small percentage of people and does not affect the suggested waiting period, or window period, of six months.)

The test result could be negative even though the infection is really there.

INCONCLUSIVE RESULTS

Sometimes test results are not definitely positive or definitely negative. If that happens, a new blood sample is drawn and the test is repeated. Many other screening tests (like those for syphilis and tuberculosis) sometimes give false-positive, false-negative, or inconclusive results.

Research scientists are working to develop new and better tests for detecting the AIDS virus. (See Chapter 8.) Even if a perfect test were found tomorrow, however, other problems could arise: (1) If a test for the AIDS virus became mandatory (that is, required), the results could devastate a person's life. (2) If HIV tests are given as a matter of routine (given to everyone in a similar group, like job applicants) without proper counseling, people could suffer needlessly. (3) If test results and medical records aren't kept private, people's jobs and home life could be harmed. Under these conditions, a test for AIDS could do more harm than good.

Mandatory Testing

"Do you think everyone in the United States should have their blood tested for the AIDS virus?"

This was a question on a survey done for *Newsweek* magazine in February 1987. Of the people who answered, more than half (52 percent) said yes. Do *you* think mandatory (required) testing for everyone is a good idea? Should a law force every man, woman, and child to be tested for the AIDS virus each year? Should you have to take a blood test for the AIDS virus before you can get married?

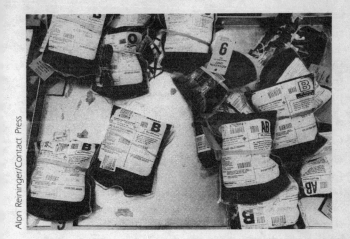

Alon Reininger/Contact Press

Donated blood such as this is now routinely tested for HIV.

Because of the problems with false-positive test results, many argue that mandatory testing for everyone could do more harm than good. There would be
tens of thousands, possibly hundreds of thousands, of
people who would be falsely labeled as HIV-positive,
even though they were not infected with HIV. And
identifying who is infected already will not necessarily
prevent the spread of the AIDS virus. Knowing test
results doesn't mean people will stop doing things
that put them or others at risk.

Some mandatory testing ideas have come from fear
and ignorance. One journalist even suggested that,
after mandatory testing, all HIV-positive people be
tattooed, to warn others. Others proposed mandatory
testing so that all HIV-positive people could be
quarantined (KWAR-un-teened), or forced to live
someplace separate from everyone else.

Such proposals discriminate against people who are sick and in need of medical and emotional support. They also discriminate against people infected with the AIDS virus who are perfectly able to live productive lives. Scientifically, such discrimination would *not* prevent the spread of AIDS. Discrimination because of the results of an HIV test is also illegal.

Other testing ideas have come from a desire to help. Counseling and help could be offered to those who test positive. The results could be used to plan for the future medical and social needs of the infected. But mandatory testing would scare away many of the people who are at high risk and most in need of this help. People would worry that the results could be used to discriminate against them.

Information about how common the virus is within a community can be obtained without linking people's names to the test results. Anonymous (that is, without names) tests can be done among groups of people in hospitals, or pregnant women in clinics, or people using family planning centers. These tests often use blood that's left over after being used for other medical purposes. No names are attached to either the blood samples or the results, although general characteristics such as age range, percentage of males and females, race, and hometown or neighborhood might

Mandatory testing would scare away many of the people who are at high risk and most in need of this help.

be known. With these group tests there is no way to identify an individual person, so no one can be discriminated against. But the person tested cannot be told the results, positive *or* negative.

In some cities, such as New York, Washington, D.C., and San Francisco, you can be tested at a clinic where anonymous testing is offered and still find out the results. You may be asked to make up a name or use a number for your blood sample. This protects you from being discriminated against, but allows only you to learn the results.

Despite the problems of mandatory testing, some agencies do have mandatory testing policies. Branches of the military, the Job Corps, and the Peace Corps all require HIV testing for people already enrolled and for all people applying for entrance. Mandatory tests are also performed on immigrants applying for U.S. citizenship and on all people who donate blood, semen, organs, or tissues. Mandatory testing has also been proposed for all pregnant women, people who have sexually transmitted diseases like syphilis, people applying for a marriage license in each of thirty-five states, and all people admitted to hospitals.

Everyone wants to find a way to stop the spread of the AIDS virus. But we need testing that (1) offers counseling both before and after; (2) is confidential, so results will not be given to anyone who does not need them for medical reasons; and (3) is voluntary, so it won't be forced on anyone. More laws that give people the right to keep their test results secret could encourage more people to get tested. And more AIDS counseling would help people learn how to live through this epidemic, whether their test results were negative or positive.

Does she or doesn't she?

People can carry the AIDS virus,
but show no symptoms.* Don't take chances.
Get tested before you become sexually involved.

*U.S. Public Health Service.

Routine Testing

HIV tests could be included as part of the "routine" evaluation and care offered by doctors, hospitals, or clinics. All people who go to clinics or hospitals in high-risk areas might be given the chance to have HIV tests—if they want the tests.

But routine testing doesn't deal with the impact of HIV test *results* on a person's life. The results of an

HIV test have much greater effect on people than the results of other routine tests, like those for strep throat or blood pressure. HIV tests should be offered only when accompanied by counseling.

Whether tests are mandatory or routine, people being tested should first understand fully the risks and benefits. Some states' laws say that no one can be tested for HIV without giving written permission. But those laws are sometimes ignored, and not all states have them. If someone ever says to you, "I'm going to run some routine blood tests on you," you should not hesitate to ask, "Blood tests for what?"

Medical tests are sometimes required if you enter a boarding school, get a new job, or apply to a live-in drug rehabilitation center or foster-care program. These tests may or may not include a test for HIV. So before you agree to have a blood sample drawn, get the facts by asking these questions:

	YES	NO
Do you require HIV testing?	—	—
Do I have to test negative to be accepted or hired?	—	—
Will you share the test results with my parents?	—	—
Will you share the test results with other people, like my school, my employer, or my insurance company?	—	—
How will I be informed of the test results?	——	
Who in your organization will know the results?	——	
Where will my records be kept?	——	
How long will my records be kept?	——	

When you have the answers, then you can decide if you want to apply. Knowing these facts beforehand will help you make a decision that is right for you.

Should *You* Be Tested?

If you have never used intravenous (IV) drugs, had sexual intercourse, or received a blood transfusion since May 1985, you are considered a "low-risk" person. People in the low-risk category don't need to have the HIV test.

But you are considered a "high-risk" person if you:

→ Inject or have ever injected drugs and shared your needle or syringe

→ Had sexual intercourse with an HIV-positive person

→ Had sexual intercourse with someone who injects drugs

→ Are a male who's had sexual intercourse with another male

→ Are the female sex partner of a male who's had sexual intercourse with another male

→ Had a blood (or a blood product) transfusion in the United States anytime between 1978 and May 1985.

People in the high-risk category are at risk of contracting the AIDS virus. But that doesn't mean they should automatically be tested. The likelihood of a high-risk person being infected depends on three factors: (1) the number of people in the area where he or she lives who are involved in high-risk activities; (2) how many times he or she has engaged in high-risk activities; and (3) how likely the virus is to be transmitted through the practiced high-risk behavior. A teenager who lives in a large city like New York, Miami, or San Francisco, who has had sexual intercourse with many partners or has a long history of repeated IV drug use, is much more likely to contract HIV than a teenager living in a small town who once had vaginal intercourse with an IV drug user. If you feel that you're a high-risk person, you should talk to a doctor or counselor. He or she will help you analyze your situation and decide if you should consider HIV testing.

A high-risk teenager might decide *not* to be tested for a number of reasons. Some teens don't think they would want—or be able—to change their behavior, no matter what the result. Knowing that one is positive or negative does not automatically stop risky behaviors. Some high-risk teens don't live near a free, anonymous, or confidential testing place. Large cities often have places (like those set up by the local departments of health) where teens can be tested in private, at no charge, and, in some states, without their parents' permission. But in smaller cities and towns it can be hard to find such a place. Most teenagers cannot afford a private doctor. In addition, many doctors wouldn't give a blood test without taking a complete medical history, which may include questions about sexual activity and drug use. Some doctors may also insist on discussing the results with a teenager's parents.

Although anonymous testing might seem like a good way to be tested, it's much better if a teenager can involve a supportive parent or adult. At anonymous testing sites, you may not get the right kind of follow-up care since the people won't even know your name. You should be counseled *before* the blood sample is drawn and have a plan for what you'll do if you're positive or if you're negative. Counseling is more likely to be offered at testing places that encourage you to come back for follow-up care.

Many high-risk teenagers might overcome their fears and be tested if they knew that the results would be kept confidential. They worry that the information about their drug use or sexuality will become known to other people. Many doctors and health professionals at clinics *will* keep your records confidential. Some states have laws that protect your right to privacy. The next chapter will tell you how to find out about the privacy laws in your state.

Sometimes high-risk teenagers don't get an HIV test because they don't know how to make the arrangements. Every day teenagers call local health departments and hospitals to ask the same kind of questions: "How can I get tested for the AIDS virus?" "Where should I go?" "What kind of test is it?" "How

---

You should be counseled *before* the blood sample is drawn and have a plan for what you'll do if you're positive or if you're negative.

Most babies with AIDS are born to mothers or fathers who have shot drugs.

Babies infected with AIDS don't live very long. How would you feel if your baby was born to die?

If you or your sex partner ever shot drugs and you want a baby, first get the AIDS test, both of you. Protect your baby. Don't get pregnant unless you're sure both of you aren't infected.

If either of you ever shot drugs or had sex with someone who did, use condoms to help protect you and your sex partner from AIDS.

And get into treatment. Now more than ever treatment could save your baby's life as well as your own.

STOP SHOOTING UP AIDS.
GET INTO DRUG TREATMENT.
CALL 1-800 662 HELP.

A Public Service of The National Institute on Drug Abuse, Department of Health and Human Services.

Help" at the back of this book. Call one of these numbers to get the information you need, or dial 411 and ask the operator for your city or state department of health.

When you call for information, tell the person who answers the phone that you are a teenager and you

---

Kits that claim you can do the test yourself at home aren't reliable.

---

want the local telephone numbers of public places that test for the AIDS virus. It's best not to call private, commercial testing places. Some do reliable work. But some may not meet the federally approved standards for HIV testing procedures, and they may give you incorrect results. Since there is no way you can tell the good from the bad, it is best to ask your local department of health to recommend a reliable testing site.

Kits that claim you can do the test yourself at home aren't reliable. The HIV test is very complicated and difficult to do exactly right. Its reliability depends on many things, including the experience of the person doing the test. Also, the kits don't have samples confirmed.

When you have the telephone numbers, call each of them to gather information. You'll find that they are not all the same. Some, for example, offer free services; others do not. Use the checklist that appears on the next two pages to make sure you get all the facts you need.

When you get the answers to these questions, you're one step closer to making a decision. Will you go to a testing site to speak to the people there and get the HIV test or not?

Information Checklist

	YES	NO
Do you usually take care of people 10 to 21 years old?	___	___
Do my parents or another adult have to come with me?	___	___
Do I need my parents' or another adult's permission to have the HIV test?	___	___
Will my parents or another adult be told the results whether I want them to be told or not?	___	___
Can I get tested free?	___	___
If not:		
How much will it cost? _____		
Do I have to pay before I get the test?	___	___
Do you give teenagers who can't afford the price a reduced rate?	___	___
Will a bill be sent in the mail for the lab test and for the office visit?	___	___
Would you put the test results in my medical records?	___	___
Will you put the test results in my medical records in the future?	___	___
Will you automatically give the results to my school?	___	___
Will you automatically give the results to my school if it asks for them?	___	___
Will you notify my sex partner(s) if I want you to?	___	___
Will you notify my partner(s) if I don't want you to?	___	___

(continued)

	YES	NO
Will you give the results to my employer?	—	—
Will you give the results to my future employers?	—	—
Will you give the results to my parents' insurance company?	—	—
Will you help me talk to my parents, sex partner(s), or other people whom I might want to tell?	—	—
Will you give the results to my insurance company in the future?	—	—
Will someone explain to me both the advantages and the disadvantages of HIV testing?	—	—
Do you give counseling before and after I take the test? [If the answer to this question is yes, be sure to ask how long the counseling session will be. You need a place that can give you a lot of time.]	—	—
Can I come back more than once to talk about whether or not to have the test? [You should be able to take your time making this decision.]	—	—
How long will I have to wait for an appointment? _____		
How long does it take to get the test results? _____		
How will I be told the results? _____		

If You Decide Not to Be Tested

Sixteen-year-old Doug has a history of IV drug use. He has decided not to get the HIV test because there isn't a free testing center near him, and the local hospital and doctors need his parents' permission. So he's decided to wait. Until Doug knows for sure, he should think he might be infected and do the things an infected person would do to protect himself and others. He should follow the guidelines for people who test positive that is outlined in the next chapter.

If you are a high-risk teen and you decide not to be tested, think about it some more. Don't just drop the subject. Like Doug, act as if you are infected. Read the information in the next chapter for teenagers who test positive. It will help you live with your decision.

Rock star Huey Lewis with a T-shirt given to him by the staff at San Francisco General Hospital. His band, Huey Lewis and the News, donated $225,000 to the hospital's AIDS training program.

If you are a high-risk teen and you decide not to be tested, think about it some more. Don't just drop the subject.

If You Decide to Be Tested

If you do decide to get the HIV test, choose the testing place that seems best for you. Call to make an appointment. Many people want this test, so you might have to wait a few weeks for your appointment. If you've used the Information Checklist above, your decision will be based on facts and on your needs. In a very short time you'll know where you stand.

5

AFTER
THE
TEST—
THEN
WHAT?

Negative Test Results

A negative test result means one of two things:

1. *You have actually been infected with HIV, but your test result reads negative.* As explained in Chapter 4, it usually takes from two weeks to six months after you're infected with HIV for your body to make enough antibodies or antigens to be detected by the most common tests. So it's possible (but unlikely) that you actually do have HIV in your body even though the test result is negative.

or

2. *You do not have HIV.* If you're a low-risk person (see page 96), you can assume your negative result is accurate because you haven't practiced risky behaviors. On the other hand, people who continue to practice high-risk behaviors continue to be at risk for getting the virus each time. So if you've done high-risk activities (see page 96), you cannot assume you are truly uninfected until another test is negative six months after your last high-risk exposure.

Jim Anderson/Woodfin Camp

A NEGATIVE TEST RESULT IS
A NEW STARTING POINT

If you haven't done anything that could expose you to the AIDS virus in the six months before the test, you can be certain that you do not have HIV. So you can use the negative result as a new starting point. It's time to think about avoiding exposure to HIV in the future.

For starters, you might want to change the way you get sexual pleasure. Keeping your partner's body fluid from entering your body will keep the virus from entering. Abstinence is the best and safest way to do this. Using condoms during sex is another way, but it is not 100 percent effective. (For more detailed information on safer-sex practices, see Chapter 2.)

If you are an IV drug user, this is the ideal time to permanently stop injecting drugs. Your negative test result—and your six months off injected drugs—gives you a clean slate for a new start. This could all be undone if you share IV needles and syringes again. Also, you'd once again suffer from not knowing whether or not you're infected. You've already taken the time and the responsibility of getting the HIV test once. If you stop injecting now, you won't have to do it again. But if you can't (or won't) stop injecting drugs, be sure to read Chapter 3 again. It explains how you can reduce the risk of getting HIV from infected needles or syringes.

If you are an IV drug user, this is the ideal time to stop injecting drugs.

Now that you know the facts about HIV, and you know how it spreads and how it doesn't spread, you can protect yourself. But the negative test result is good only for as long as you avoid high-risk behaviors. If you have unprotected sexual intercourse with a new or different partner, or if you share IV needles and syringes, you should consider having another test. No one can say how often the test should be repeated. But if you practice risky behaviors frequently, you might want to be tested every six months.

Positive Test Results

A positive test result means one of two things:

1. *You have not actually been infected with HIV, but your test result reads positive.* If this is the first time you've taken the test, it could be a false-positive result. If you are a high-risk person (see page 96), it is unlikely to be a false-positive result, since the tests are more than 99 percent accurate for high-risk people. But if you're a low-risk person, then it might be a false-positive result. Find out for sure by contacting the testing place. Ask if your blood sample was tested twice with ELISA and if it was also given the Western blot test or an antigen test. You can also ask for a new test.

or

2. *You have been infected with HIV.* If this positive test is the result of repeated ELISA tests plus the Western blot test or another confirmatory test, it means that you almost certainly have been infected with HIV. (This is not always the case with newborn babies. The presence of antibodies means that the mother is infected, but not necessarily the baby.)

If you do have HIV, it does not mean that you have AIDS.

If you do have HIV, it does not mean that you have AIDS. Most people with a positive test result do *not* have AIDS at the time of testing. Some researchers believe that more than 9 out of every 10 people infected with HIV will eventually develop AIDS. Twenty to 30 percent of infected people progress from asymptomatic (no symptoms) HIV to AIDS within five years. But a small fraction of people have remained well after nine years of HIV infection. Until more long-term studies are completed, it's impossible to say how long an HIV-infected person can remain asymptomatic. It's also impossible to say how mild or severe the course of the infection will be.

Once you know for certain that you've been infected with HIV, you should find a place to receive emotional support and medical care. You should also know your legal rights. The following sections will guide you through these steps.

Guidelines for People with HIV

EMOTIONAL NEEDS

No one can know exactly how he or she would feel if told of a positive result. But many people with HIV say the same thing when they first hear the news: "This can't be true."

It's very common for people to deny that they're infected. Kari wanted to believe it was a lie, a mistake, or even a bad dream—anything but the truth. She tried to shut the whole thing out of her mind and pretend it never happened. She denied it to her family and friends. Soon she convinced herself it wasn't true. This may have made Kari's fears easier to bear. But by denying the truth, she was also denying herself the emotional and physical care she needed. The AIDS virus will not go away just because you ignore it. It's best to face it early, because there's a lot you can do to keep yourself as healthy as possible, both emotionally and physically.

Actress Elizabeth Taylor testifying before a Senate subcommittee in Washington, D.C. Ms. Taylor asked the Senate to increase the amount of money the government spends to find a cure for AIDS.

Facing the fact that you're infected with a potentially fatal infection is very difficult. The first step is to talk with a counselor. Sharing your feelings with someone who has worked with people like you and who knows the facts will help you sort out your fears. This can help you make decisions that are right for you.

If the positive test result makes you feel overwhelmed, break down your situation into smaller pieces that you can deal with. Rather than thinking about the next 10 years, think about what you can do today, and then tomorrow. By taking one thing at a time, one day at a time, you can see that there are many parts of your life that are under your control. HIV does not leave you powerless. A counselor can help you learn how to take charge of your life and live with the virus rather than spend your time waiting to die from it.

"I'm so scared."   Having an infection that cannot be cured is terribly frightening. When Tom got his positive result, his whole body began to shake. "I still shake every time I think about having HIV," says Tom. "I'm scared because I have the AIDS virus. But I'm also scared because I don't know if or when I'll develop AIDS. It's not knowing for sure that scares me the most."

There's a lot you can do to keep yourself as healthy as possible, both emotionally and physically.

It's okay to be scared. Almost everyone with HIV is. As you begin to deal with this fear, you should constantly remind yourself that you are the same person today that you were before you got the positive test result. You still have friends and hobbies. You still have most of the same day-to-day concerns you always had. Now you also have decisions to make about handling this infection. An AIDS counselor can help you do these things.

"Why me?" People with HIV who search for the answer to this question often end up blaming themselves and feeling guilty. Jessica thought she deserved to have the AIDS virus. "If I'd listened to my parents and stayed away from drugs," she said, "this wouldn't have happened to me. I guess I'm being punished." Jessica needs to spend time talking to a counselor. She needs to learn that this virus can't tell the difference between "bad" and "good" people. It infects all kinds of people. What's more, *no one* deserves to get HIV. And *no one* deserves to get AIDS.

"I'm so angry!" People often express their fear, confusion, and hurt through anger. Some turn their anger outward and seem hostile, nasty, cruel, or irre-

---

This virus can't tell the difference between "bad" and "good" people. What's more, *no one* deserves to get HIV. And *no one* deserves to get AIDS.

---

sponsible. Others turn their anger toward themselves, or toward whoever exposed them to the virus, or toward the world that "dealt them such a bad deal." They often withdraw from the people who could help them. They blame themselves and then punish themselves by becoming isolated or self-destructive.

Anger is a natural reaction. But if it makes you turn away from help, or hurt yourself or someone else, then your anger isn't helping you face the problem. Being able to show your anger and talk about it with a counselor is an important step toward helping yourself.

People who test positive for HIV need a lot of emotional support. When you first get the news of a positive result, talk to counselors and doctors about your feelings. Let them know if you're scared, angry, or lonely. Most people feel some or all of these emotions. Prepare a list of questions. It's okay to go back to the counselor with the same questions. Go over and over the information until you understand it all. There are many facts to talk about and many feelings to share.

You'll also need emotional support as you try to deal with your feelings in the weeks and months to come. You might ask your counselor to help you find a support group for people with HIV that can help you with the wide range of emotions you'll experience. Although it's helpful to have supportive friends and family, it's also helpful to talk with people in support groups who are not emotionally attached to you. They can help you accept your infection and get on with your life. They can help you make decisions about school, work, where to live, what to do in your free time, and what to tell your friends and family.

They can also help you think ahead about things like getting married and having children; about employment and finances; and about emotional and physical health care.

WHOM SHOULD YOU TELL?

The first difficult decision you'll face is, who should know about your condition? It's especially hard to decide when you have no symptoms. One part of you may not want to tell anyone, but another part of you needs to talk about it. You may feel like telling all your friends or all the people in your neighborhood, school, or workplace because it weighs so heavily on your mind, and you can't stand keeping it to yourself. But it's best to first talk with a counselor about whom to tell. People may react with less understanding and compassion than you think they will.

Talking to a counselor is helpful in the beginning, but then you'll need somebody who can be there for you every day. When possible, that somebody should be your parents. If you're a minor (under legal age) and are living at home, then your parents are still responsible for you. Even if you're not living at home, your parents are probably the first adults you should consider talking to. If that's not possible, tell another adult who's important to you—someone who can help you with the complicated choices and adjustments you'll have to make.

If you've told your parents about your decision to be tested for HIV, then they're already prepared to hear the results. But if they don't know about that decision, the counselors at the testing place can help you decide the best way to tell them. Some alternatives are:

The first difficult decision you'll face is, who should know about your condition?

---

1. With your permission, the counselors can tell your parents when you're not present. This should not be done by phone or by letter but in person. This gives your parents a chance to adjust to the idea and talk about their own feelings before they talk with you about what to do next.

2. Your counselor can call or write to your parents to set up a time for all of you to meet. Then you and/or the counselor can explain the test result and what it means. This gives you the chance to speak for yourself. It also provides for backup support and expertise.

3. You can go home and tell your parents by yourself. This gives you privacy. It gives your parents a chance to react without worrying about being upset in front of strangers. If you choose this method, be sure to give your parents the telephone number of your counselor or doctor. They, too, will then know someone who can answer their questions and provide emotional support.

MEDICAL CARE

If you test HIV-positive, you'll need to find a doctor to give you medical care. If you don't want to go to your family doctor, ask the counselor where you were tested to refer you to a local clinic or hospital that has

experience helping young people with HIV. You
should get ongoing medical care because:

→ You'll need special medical attention. You may
  react differently, for example, to common infections or immunizations (like the measles vaccine)
  from people who are not infected.

→ You are vulnerable to infections and cancers that
  uninfected people rarely get. (See Chapter 1.)
  These illnesses need to be diagnosed and treated
  early. Some of these rare infections can now be
  prevented by special treatments. (See Chapter 6.)

→ You may get more extreme or prolonged infections from common viruses (like mononucleosis)
  or from bacteria (like the one that causes tuberculosis), which are treated more easily in uninfected people.

→ When you get common illnesses like acne, the
  flu, or a strep throat, you may not respond to the
  medication as you would if you were uninfected.

→ You'll need to see a doctor right away if you get
  any unexplained symptoms.

→ Your doctor may want to prescribe one of the
  medical treatments that might help you to live
  longer.

→ Before you consider having children, you should
  talk with a doctor or nurse. If you or your partner
  is already pregnant when you get a positive test
  result, you'll need to know about the special risks
  to the fetus and its mother. Both are in danger of
  getting illnesses caused by the infection plus the

other changes caused by pregnancy. You'll need to think about these new risks when you decide whether to continue the pregnancy.

LEGAL RIGHTS

After you tell your parents, you should give a great deal of thought to who else should be told about your test results. You know that casual contact doesn't spread AIDS. But many others don't know or won't accept that, so they may be afraid of you. They may do and say things that make it hard for you to live a normal life. Knowing your legal rights may help you decide who does and who does not need to know.

The laws about people with HIV and AIDS can differ from state to state, and they change quite often. So before you make any decisions about whom to tell, you and your parents should discuss contacting a lawyer. If you can't afford a lawyer, check the telephone directory or call information (411) and ask for the number of your local Civil Liberties Union, Legal Aid Society, or AIDS hotlines. Someone there will almost certainly be able to help you.

1. School rights: If you get a positive test result, you do not have to quit school. The Centers for Disease Control, an agency of the federal government, says that students with HIV or AIDS should be allowed to attend school as long as they can, unless they pose a risk to others. This is not a law; it's a suggestion. But most states agree with this policy. School officials decide each case individually. To help make these decisions, many cities have set up special committees or groups. These groups usually include people from

Ryan White talking with classmates at Hamilton Heights High School in Indiana, where his infection with the AIDS virus has been well accepted by the students and teachers.

the local health department and board of education, as well as community representatives and health-care professionals.

If you have no symptoms, there's no reason for you to be kept out of school. In fact, *you* bear the greater health risk. You may be at risk for getting common infections from the other kids at school. If your immune system has been weakened by HIV, it might not be able to handle these illnesses.

If you get a positive test result, you do not have to quit school.

You and your parents will have to decide if anyone at your school needs to know about your test result. This is a personal decision that depends mostly on your health. But here are some reasons you might want the school authorities to know:

→ If you're not feeling well and want to go home, or if you're often absent because of illness, someone at school should know the reason.

→ You may need to make some changes in your schedule when you're not feeling up to certain activities. Or you may have to leave school for medical tests or treatment.

→ When the subject of HIV and AIDS is taught in your health class, the teacher should be aware of your infection. He or she can then handle the discussion with greater compassion and sensitivity to your situation.

2. Employment rights: People with HIV or AIDS sometimes have trouble keeping their jobs. Some have been fired or forced to take an unpaid leave of absence. So people with HIV have to be very careful whom they tell. Employers may find out about an employee's infection through insurance or medical records or through company physical exams. If your employer finds out, there are federal laws that protect you from job discrimination. If you're physically able to perform your job, you cannot legally be fired or demoted. If you are, call a lawyer.

3. Ambulance, doctor, and hospital services: The law says that you cannot be denied an ambulance ride, hospital emergency-room treatment, or admittance to the hospital. The laws are less clear, however, on a hospital's responsibility in situations that aren't emergencies. In some states, hospital staff can refuse to admit people with HIV or AIDS for hospital treatment.

The American Medical Association has said that doctors can't refuse to treat people with HIV or AIDS. But some doctors or dentists may still be reluctant to care for you. It's best if you can find a doctor who *wants* to care for you rather than one who feels forced to.

4. Insurance rights: If you're a minor (under 18), your health-care costs may be covered by your parents' health insurance. Check to be sure. Making a

Alon Reininger/Contact Press

Actress Susan Sarandon at the "Fighting for Our Lives" AIDS rally in New York City. She became involved with the AIDS issue when a friend of hers died of the disease. She is pictured here with Bob Cecchi, who belongs to an organization called Men with AIDS.

claim may cause you additional problems. Your parents would have to know about your infection, because they have to sign the forms. If you ask the insurance company to pay for your HIV- or AIDS-related care, that information may later be used against you. When you sign a release for your medical records, sometimes the information can be shared with your employer, landlord, creditors, banks, or other insurers or with government agencies. On the other hand, if you give the insurance company false information (if, for example, you change the diagnosis from AIDS to some other illness), they may take away your policy or deny your claims if the truth comes out.

If you don't use, or don't have, insurance, you may have trouble paying the cost of your health care. Public assistance programs can help you. Medicaid benefits are now available to some people with HIV or AIDS. You may qualify on your own if you're 18 years old or if you're a minor who is either a parent or living on your own or supporting yourself. Call your local department of social services to get more information.

5. Housing rights: The same civil rights laws that protect you against job discrimination usually protect you from being evicted from your house or apartment. If your landlord finds out about your illness and tries to make you or your family move out, call a lawyer immediately.

6. Alien rights: If you are not a citizen of the United States, you face additional problems. If you apply for citizenship, you'll be tested for HIV. If you test positive, your citizenship request can be turned down. U.S. immigration laws say that if you're a drug abuser or a man who has sex with other men or someone who

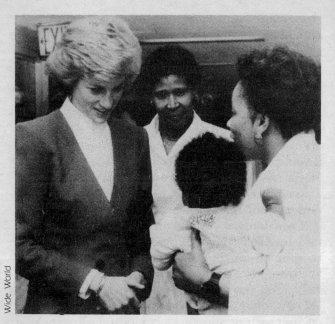

Princess Diana with one of the many young children with AIDS whom she held, talked to, and cuddled at Harlem Hospital during her three-day visit to New York City in February 1989.

may become "a burden to the state" (if you won't be able to pay your medical bills, for example), you can be kept out of this country or sent back to the country of your birth. It is important for you to get expert legal advice, because the immigration laws are often difficult to understand by yourself.

These are legal problems people with the AIDS virus often face. In time you may face others. But under any circumstances, if you're discriminated

Under any circumstances, if you're discriminated against in any way because of your illness, call a lawyer for help and advice.

against in any way because of your illness, call a lawyer for help and advice.

PRACTICAL GUIDELINES

If your HIV test is positive, you should follow these suggestions:

1. Abstain from sexual intercourse. Or use a condom during sexual intercourse or oral sex, so that vaginal fluids and semen are not passed from you to another person.

2. Never share IV drug needles and syringes. Even if only very little blood is left in them, they can transmit the virus.

3. Consider postponing having children until more is known about the risks to you and to the unborn child. (An infected woman has a 30 to 65 percent chance of passing the virus on to her baby.)

4. Do not donate blood, sperm, or any part of your body.

5. If you cut yourself and get blood (or semen or saliva) on clothes or furniture, clean it with soap and water. Then clean again with alcohol, a disinfectant, or water mixed with household bleach (½ cup of bleach to 4½ cups of water). Afterwards, be sure to wash your hands with soap and running water. Dry cleaning can also kill the virus.

6. Tell your past and present sexual partners, or anyone with whom you have shared IV needles and syringes, that they might have been infected with the virus. If you don't want to tell them yourself, speak with a health professional or someone from the local department of health. He or she can inform them (without revealing your name) that they may have been exposed to HIV.

7. See a doctor for a complete checkup.

8. To improve your chances of staying healthy, avoid drugs and heavy alcohol use. Eat a balanced diet. Avoid extra stress and activities that might exhaust you.

All persons have stress in their lives. People with HIV infection have extra stresses. Be sure to make room in your day for activities that are fun or pleasurable to help balance your life.

Questions and Answers

Question: I belong to a dating club that tests applicants for HIV. Only people who test negative are allowed to join. Am I protected from getting the AIDS virus if I have sexual intercourse with only the people in this club?

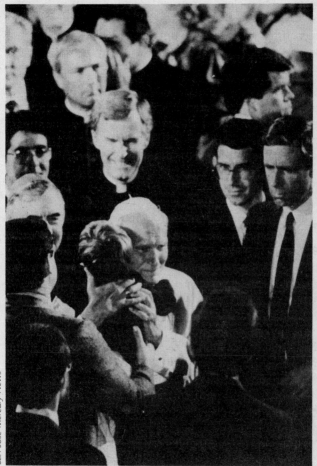

San Jose Mercury News

Pope John Paul II hugs five-year-old Brendan O'Rourke, who has AIDS.

Answer: No. Having a negative test is not an insurance policy. It *may* mean that a member is not infected. But it may also mean that there were not enough HIV antibodies or antigens in his or her blood to be detected at the time of the testing. If a person practices risky behaviors, he or she can become infected at any time after taking the test. Also, some clubs and individuals print phony ID cards or make up false laboratory results.

Question: Should I tell my dentist that I have tested positive for HIV?

Answer: Yes. But not all health professionals know the facts about HIV or are willing to care for HIV-positive people. The American Medical Association has stated that doctors cannot refuse to treat HIV-positive people. The American Dental Association, however, has said that if a dentist isn't able to care for HIV-positive people, he or she doesn't have to. But the dentist must refer infected patients to another dentist who will care for them.

Question: My boyfriend and I both tested positive for the AIDS virus. Do we still have to use a condom during sex?

Answer: Yes. Because you and your boyfriend have HIV, your immune systems may not be working properly. If either of you now gets a sexually transmitted disease like syphilis, gonorrhea, or herpes, these infections may be harder to treat and you may develop AIDS more easily from your HIV infection. So your boyfriend should wear a condom to prevent this. He should also wear a condom during intercourse to avoid your getting pregnant with a baby that may be born with HIV.

6

TREATMENT

AIDS Is Difficult to Treat

There are many ways to diagnose and treat each of the AIDS-related diseases. But HIV remains in the body. So even when an illness is diagnosed and relieved, other illnesses will occur over time. So the search for new and better treatments continues.

The two most challenging difficulties in treating HIV and AIDS are:

1. *The virus itself is changing all the time*. Different forms of the virus have been found. The differences between each form are small, but the virus differs from person to person and changes over time, even within one person.

There are also different types of HIV. HIV-1 is the name for the virus that was first linked to AIDS. In 1985 a similar virus, called HIV-2, was found in West Africa. It also has been found recently in the United States. (HIV-2 may cause less serious problems than HIV-1.) There is also another type, called HTLV-1, which commonly causes leukemia. So far HTLV-1 is found more often in Japan than in the United States.

2. *HIV is difficult to control*. It invades cells in various parts of the body. It can get into the cells of the central nervous system and affect the brain or into the cells of the intestinal tract. It can infect the vagina or the penis. It can get into the blood by infecting the cells of the immune system. Some of these cells can carry the infection from one part of the body to another. The only way to get rid of the virus would be to get rid of the cells. Since these cells are vital to life, this isn't possible.

The only way to get rid of the virus would be to get rid of the cells. Since these cells are vital to life, this isn't possible.

Despite these difficulties, several new drugs have been developed that may slow the pace of AIDS-related diseases. Older medicines are now being changed to make their effects last longer. Drug companies are also experimenting with new ways to deliver the medicines. Some are now available in forms that can be swallowed. Others are in an aerosol form that can be sprayed through the mouth and into the lungs.

In the past, the process for developing, testing, and approving drugs was very slow. The U.S. Food and Drug Administration (FDA) has strict guidelines for judging drugs before they can be given to the public. Sometimes this process can take several years. But in response to the urgent needs of people with AIDS, the FDA has a new system that speeds up the testing of new drugs. This change has opened the door to better treatments for thousands of people with HIV-related illnesses or AIDS.

Medical Treatments Being Developed

There are four different kinds of medical treatments being developed. Each has a purpose very different from the others, but they are all important.

Jim Anderson/Woodfin Camp

VACCINES

The job of a vaccine is to protect uninfected people. As a child you were probably vaccinated against diseases such as measles, mumps, and whooping cough. Even though you've never actually had these diseases, if you received the correct vaccine dose your body has produced antibodies that will protect you if you are exposed to them.

In preparing a vaccine, a small amount of virus or bacteria is changed or weakened. Sometimes a part of it is manufactured. It is then either given orally or injected into the muscle or skin. This form of the virus or bacteria doesn't cause full symptoms of the disease. But the immune system, thinking the body is in danger, manufactures antibodies to fight off the virus or bacteria. These antibodies circulate through the blood and protect against future infection from that virus or bacteria.

Unfortunately, an HIV vaccine won't be available until at least the mid-1990s. There are many unanswered questions. Scientists still don't know which part of the virus will cause the body to produce the most antibodies. It's especially confusing because the body makes its own antibodies in reaction to HIV infection. But these don't offer resistance the way antibodies do for other kinds of infection.

Even when a vaccine is developed, there will still be many other questions. Since injecting some forms of HIV into the body might result in AIDS, who should be asked to test the vaccine? How much immunity will it offer? How long will the protection last? How many doses will be necessary? Who should be vaccinated, and at what age? These and many more questions need to be answered before a vaccine can be offered.

ANTIVIRAL DRUGS

Antiviral drugs attack the virus in an infected person. Some antiviral drugs being developed may block the virus before it can do damage to other healthy cells. Others may stop the virus from multiplying within cells. This would help prevent HIV-related diseases, which are often fatal.

It's difficult to find antiviral drugs to fight HIV. Even if the production of new HIV could be blocked, the virus would still be in the infected cells. Drug treatments for HIV must therefore be taken for the

---

Unfortunately, an HIV vaccine won't be available until at least the mid-1990s. There are many unanswered questions.

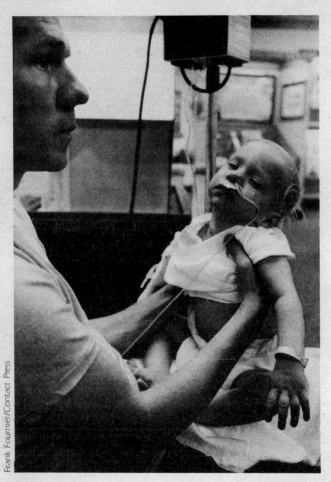

Frank Fournier/Contact Press

Patrick Burk holding his son Dwight. Mr. Burk, a hemophiliac, had gotten HIV from a transfusion and passed the virus to his wife, who then transmitted it to their son Dwight while she was either pregnant or breast-feeding. When this picture was taken in 1985, both Patrick and Dwight had developed AIDS. They have both since died.

full length of a person's life. So the drugs must have few side effects and must be able to be taken conveniently (not too often in a day and preferably by mouth rather than by injection). Another problem is that HIV can pass from the bloodstream into the brain. It is difficult to develop drugs strong enough to reach the brain cells without doing damage to other parts of the body.

Antiviral drugs are being developed to stop HIV at every point of action. When these drugs are tested and approved, doctors will have better weapons to fight off the virus.

IMMUNE BOOSTERS

Immune boosters help strengthen the body's immune system. They help the immune system fight off opportunistic diseases. They also help block the destruction caused by viruses, bacteria, and fungi. The body makes a chemical, called interferon (in-ter-FEER-ahn), that does this naturally. But when HIV infects a cell, the immune system can't make enough interferon to protect the body. A type of interferon is now being given to infected people as an experiment. Interferon attacks the virus when the cell releases new virus particles. So it may be able to stop the spread of HIV throughout the body.

DIAGNOSIS AND TREATMENT OF DISEASES AND INFECTIONS

Early diagnosis is the key to treating AIDS-related diseases and infections. Doctors can treat many of these infections once they develop. In some cases, they can prevent them from developing.

The treatments for many of these diseases have been available for years. But they weren't working as effectively for people with the AIDS virus as they should have been. An infected person's immune system can't fight off opportunistic infections. These infections are more serious and last longer in people with AIDS than in uninfected people. Researchers have improved the drug treatments so they can be given for longer periods of time, in stronger doses, and with fewer side effects. In the past, these drugs could only lessen the symptoms or illnesses after they appeared. But now they can be used to prevent them from occurring. It's not known if these drugs will actually prolong the lives of infected people. But they can improve the quality of their lives and help them feel healthier.

Available Treatments

ANTIVIRAL MEDICINE—ZIDOVUDINE (AZT)

At this time, the only drug formally approved by the Food and Drug Administration for people with AIDS is a pill or a liquid called zidovudine, or AZT. AZT keeps an infected cell from producing more HIV. It gives the immune system a chance to fight off the diseases that affect people with AIDS.

People who take AZT generally feel much better. These people have a strengthened immune system. Many regain lost weight and have fewer fevers and infections.

AZT is not a cure for AIDS. But it is improving the lives of many infected people. Its use is continually

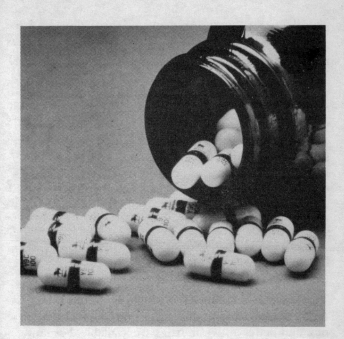

AZT keeps an infected cell from producing more HIV.

expanding. At first it was given only to those in the final stages of disease. Then it was found to be more effective when used earlier in the course of AIDS. Now it's being offered to asymptomatic HIV-infected people. This will enable scientists to study its ability to fight off opportunistic diseases and to keep HIV-infected people as healthy as possible.

There are some problems with AZT. In many people it produces side effects. These can range from nausea to dangerous effects on the bone marrow or organs like the liver. Also, the effects of AZT last only a few hours at a time. So it has to be given continuously by vein or every four to six hours by mouth. AZT affects healthy cells as well as infected cells, so there may be other possible dangers as well.

AZT has improved the quality of life for many people with AIDS. It has improved their health and reduced problems like weight loss, weakness, and fevers. It has also helped to reduce the number of diseases and infections. For others, unfortunately, its side effects make it unbearable. But AZT is only the first drug of its kind to be approved for use. As research continues there will probably be others that will work in different ways and cause fewer side effects.

DIAGNOSIS AND TREATMENT
OF OPPORTUNISTIC DISEASES

The best way to fight AIDS would be to block HIV, the virus that causes it. But that won't be possible until new and better antiviral drugs are available. For now, early identification and treatment of opportunistic diseases are the main source of hope for people with AIDS. The table on the next page lists the four different types of opportunistic diseases. It also lists the diagnostic tools used to identify each one, and the drugs available for their treatment.

AZT has improved the quality of life for many people with AIDS. For others, unfortunately, its side effects make it unbearable.

OPPORTUNISTIC DISEASES	DIAGNOSTIC TESTS	EXAMPLES OF TREATMENT
Pneumocystis carinii	Sputum test or biopsy (phlegm is coughed up or cells are taken from the lungs and analyzed on a laboratory slide or culture)	Antibiotics: Trimethoprim sulfameth-oxazole or Pentamidine
Tuberculosis (TB)	Skin test Culture of blood, body fluid, or tissue Sputum test Slide smear test	Antibiotics: Isoniazid and Rifampin
Kaposi's sarcoma Lymphoma	Bone marrow sample X-rays Ultrasound Blood tests Biopsy Tests of tissues, cells, or body fluids	Chemotherapy and radiation
Herpes Cytomegalovirus (CMV)	Antibody or antigen test of blood, body fluids, or tissue	Antivirals: Acyclovir and Gangcyclovir

Psychological Problems of People with HIV or AIDS

The health of your body and of your mind are closely connected. You can't treat one fully without considering the other. Often the treatment of psychological problems helps physical problems. This is especially true with HIV infection.

When HIV invades the brain cells, it causes brain damage. The symptoms may include disorientation, confusion, loss of balance and/or coordination, paralysis of parts of the body, personality changes, depression, and dementia (dih-MEN-chuh)—a loss of mental powers that affects a person's judgment, memory,

Lynne Weinstein/Woodfin Camp

and reasoning abilities. These symptoms may be the first signs of illness in some infected people. (Dementia usually occurs in the late stages of AIDS, when the person has only a few more months to live.)

Even when HIV doesn't invade the brain cells, it can still cause emotional reactions. These range from physical symptoms to severe depression and fear to suicide.

A wide range of health-care professionals can treat the emotional problems that people with the AIDS virus face. Your regular medical doctor can help you decide who is best for you to see. Some possibilities include a neurologist, a psychologist, a social worker, or a psychiatrist who is specially trained to help people your age.

Once the central nervous system is infected by the virus, there is little hope of total recovery. But treatment programs and medications can help control the symptoms. These treatments can solve a lot of common problems. They help people function as best they can for as long as possible.

Treatment programs that combine therapy (in-depth discussions) and medication can be very helpful. Therapy sessions can be one-on-one with your doctor. There are also a number of group situations. Some therapy groups are specifically for people with HIV infections or with AIDS. Others are for parents of infected babies. Still others are for family members or loved ones of people who are infected and for people who have lost a loved one to AIDS. The "Call for Help" section in the back of this book lists resources that are available to help infected people deal with the psychological pain that can be caused by the AIDS virus.

Psychological Problems
of Uninfected People

There are a number of AIDS-related psychological problems that affect many uninfected people.

There are "worried-well" people who are not infected but who are suffering emotionally. Some are worried because they have practiced risky behaviors. They may become so worried about being infected that they actually get physical illnesses. Luis, for example, doesn't have AIDS. But because he once had sexual intercourse with another man, he's afraid he might be infected. He's worried himself into having frequent headaches and losing weight. His fear of discussing this sexual experience keeps Luis from getting counseling that would help him sort out his concerns about HIV from his concerns about his sexuality.

Other "worried-well" people are low-risk people who live with the unrealistic fear that they will become infected through casual contact. This keeps them from living a full or normal life. Sometimes teenagers' fears get so strong that they miss out on a lot of normal, healthy activities. Tamara, for example, is a low-risk person who doesn't have AIDS. But she's still very worried about getting the virus. She won't touch the handrail on the stairs in her apartment building. She won't use public telephones or rest rooms. She no longer eats in restaurants, and her body begins to shake with panic when she's in large crowds.

Some people who have a negative test result wrongly think that, since they tried risky behaviors and didn't get the AIDS virus, they might be immune to it. Others are so relieved that they celebrate by practicing the same behaviors that put them at risk in

---

Some people worry because they have practiced risky behaviors. They may become so worried about being infected that they actually get physical illnesses.

---

the first place. Still others who get a negative result can't get over the anxiety. They continue to worry that the test was wrong or that they might still become infected in the future. They worry so much that it disrupts their lives.

The worries and fears of uninfected people can be diagnosed and treated like those of people who have HIV or AIDS. If you want to talk to someone about your concerns, call your doctor or local department of health and find out where counseling is available. Or go to the places where the HIV tests are done. These sites usually have a trained counselor. When you call or visit one of these sites, however, don't let yourself be pressured into having an HIV test. It is not necessarily the solution to your fears. The decision to have or not to have a test for HIV is different from the decision to discuss your feelings about HIV and AIDS.

Nutritional Care

When people have a disease that may be fatal, eating the right foods may not seem too important. But nutrition plays a crucial role in living with AIDS.

AIDS-related illnesses often cause malnutrition

problems. People with opportunistic infections and diseases may lose too much weight too fast. They might have lost their appetites, or they can't eat, or they have long-lasting diarrhea and fever. As they lose nutrients, their immune systems become even weaker and more open to illnesses and infections.

Extreme weight loss can also affect a person's self-image. When a person sees himself or herself "wasting away," death can appear unavoidable. There may seem little reason to fight back. He or she may also feel very unattractive and different from other people. Although improved nutrition will not cure AIDS-related illnesses, it can make the person physically and emotionally stronger throughout the course of the disease.

Nutritional treatment for people with AIDS aims to maintain normal body weight and necessary nutrients. Most doctors and nurses know how to do this. Trained dieticians and nutrition experts can also create a dietary program that will meet the nutritional requirements of people with AIDS, at home or in the hospital.

Most infected people need the same nutrients from the same basic food groups as uninfected people. A nutritional counselor may decide that some people with AIDS-related illnesses need increased amounts of particular nutrients. But a person with AIDS could be harmed if food choices are severely limited or exaggerated. This is especially true for a teenager with AIDS. During puberty, body weight usually doubles and height increases by 20 to 30 percent. During this time the body needs extra protein and nutrients, like calcium and iron. A diet that does not include these could do further damage to the infected teen's health.

People all over America are helping people with AIDS by bringing them food. Some do it for a family member or a few friends. Others prepare, deliver, and serve hot meals every day to people with AIDS. This offers people with AIDS two kinds of treatment: food to help keep their bodies strong and friendship to help keep their spirits high. Both are vital in the fight against AIDS.

Social Support

Social support is unavailable to many of the people who need it. Some people with AIDS have been abandoned by their family and friends. Others can't get proper medical care because the doctors in their town are reluctant to take care of them. Still others are

Movie and theater celebrities, including Lily Tomlin, Glenn Close, Sam Waterston, and Bernadette Peters, at an AIDS benefit for Ryan White (front row, center) in New York City, 1986.

suffering from loneliness. They have no one to help them, no one to do simple things like bring them food or dial the phone. Most people with AIDS suffer extreme emotional pain because they don't get enough support or love. Two days before she died, Laurie wrote about this kind of pain in her diary: "It seems I start every day with the same hope. I'm not hoping for a cure, and I'm not hoping for less pain. I'm hoping that someone will walk through my door with open arms and hug me and talk to me. Someone—anyone—who will touch me and make me feel like a human being again."

Treatment for this pain can come from people like you. You can strengthen a person's desire to live and improve the quality of someone's life. You can help give a person with HIV or AIDS emotional strength by simply showing interest, support, and compassion. You do this directly when you offer friendship or help to the people with HIV or AIDS in your school or neighborhood. You do this indirectly when you explain the facts about AIDS to your family and friends. In these ways, you can be part of the treatment program for people with HIV and AIDS.

Two days before she died, Laurie wrote in her diary: "It seems I start every day with the same hope. I'm hoping that someone will walk through my door with open arms and hug me and talk to me."

Unproven Treatments

Many treatments for HIV-related illnesses and AIDS have proved effective through scientific studies. But there is also a whole assortment of unproven remedies that range from harmless herbal teas to psychic healers to dangerous toxic injections. Some treatments that have not been approved for use in the United States are available in other countries. Often they are purchased in these countries and then brought back to this country. For example, there are two experimental drugs (isoprinosine and ribavirin) that are sold legally and without a prescription in Mexico. Most American doctors think it's unwise for people with AIDS to give themselves these medicines without knowing about their use, safety, and side effects. Yet doctors on the West Coast say that 25 to 30 percent of adult AIDS patients have given themselves one or both of the drugs available in Mexico.

Drug researchers are also concerned about unproven drugs. It's difficult for them to know which treatments are effective if people involved in drug trials compromise (or change) the results. Drug trials study the effectiveness of a drug. The results are compromised if the people involved secretly take unproven medicines, which can affect the body in many ways.

In 1988, 400 health professionals and educators gathered for the National Health Fraud Conference in Kansas City. They discussed a list of so-called AIDS therapies that are sold in America. These include pond scum in intravenous solutions, herbal preparations, hydrogen peroxide injections, Japanese mushrooms, a soybean derivative, and a hand lotion made with a chemical used in photography. The health of-

Overheard by the lockers . . .

AIDS? Alex has AIDS? You mean Jamie's big brother Alex?

That's what he's got. Jamie and I talked at the hospital. Alex won't be going back to college . . . at least, it doesn't look that way now.

Is he gay?

He's really sick, that's what he is, you jerk!

Weren't you scared to be with him?

Jamie's my friend. So's Alex.

Did you *touch* him?

He was pretty shook up. I hugged him, sure. And don't give me that look—you *can't* get AIDS from hugging a friend! I'm going back to see him when he goes home next week—you coming?

From *Teens & AIDS: Playing It Safe* (© 1987, 1988 American Council of Life Insurance and Health Insurance Association of America)

ficials are concerned that people who use these un-proven "remedies" may not seek the treatments that have proved effective. This could lead to further suffering and perhaps premature death.

Until 1988 there were no special treatment programs for teenagers with HIV. The first drug trials were for adults over the age of 18. Then special arrangements were made for research studies on the medicines used to treat children up to the age of 13. Plans are now being made to include teenagers.

The best approach to health care for people with HIV or AIDS is through a combination of the available approved treatments. These treatments can prevent or control the direct effects of HIV, illnesses, and infections. They can also ease the emotional strain of the diseases, improve an infected person's nutritional state, and boost his or her spirits through social support.

7

AIDS
IN
THE
FUTURE

Predictions

Medical authorities have made many predictions about the future of the AIDS epidemic:

→ According to the Centers for Disease Control (CDC), the reported number of people with AIDS in the United States will rise from 83,000 at the end of 1988 to 270,000 in 1991, and to 450,000 in 1993.

→ The CDC also predicts that AIDS will kill between 142,000 and 201,000 Americans by the year 1991.

→ With 450 new AIDS cases reported each week, the Public Health Service Report predicts that AIDS will be one of the top 10 causes of death by 1991.

These predictions are based on the spread of the virus so far and on the treatments currently available for infected people. But the actual future course of the AIDS epidemic depends on a number of other factors.

Testing

Medical researchers around the world are working to develop better tests for detecting HIV. In the future, doctors will have several testing options:

→ The HIV antibody tests that are currently used will be improved. Better tests will decrease the number of false-negative, false-positive, and inconclusive results.

→ Antigen tests that test directly for the presence of HIV will be more readily available. They will be used to tell how quickly the virus is spreading through the body, how much of the virus is in the body, and how well the immune system is coping. In July 1988 a new antigen test called PCR (for *p*olymerase *c*hain *r*eaction) was announced. It can detect HIV before the body starts to make antibodies, even if the virus is hidden in the cell. This test may show whether a newborn baby who has HIV antibodies is actually infected.

→ Viral culture tests will be refined. These laboratory tests enable medical workers to actually grow the virus from the cells or body fluids of people who are infected with HIV. But right now they are time-consuming and expensive. Few places have the necessary equipment or staff. And the virus doesn't always grow in the culture.

These antigen and viral culture tests are being refined. In the future they'll be used along with the antibody tests to form a battery, or combination, of tests. Together these tests will make it easier to diagnose who is infected, to track the course of HIV, and to determine the effectiveness of various treatments.

Medical Treatments

Drug manufacturers and government laboratories are working to find medical treatments to slow the pace of, and lower the death toll from, the AIDS epidemic. Some are looking for a vaccine to protect the uninfected. Others are testing antiviral drugs that will attack the virus in infected people. These efforts may

Wide World

Top personalities from the world of dance announcing a special benefit performance, called "Dance for Life," to raise $1.4 million for AIDS research. Pictured, from left to right, are New York City Ballet Artistic Director Peter Martins; Dance Theater of Harlem Artistic Director Arthur Mitchell; Laura Dean, artistic director of Laura Dean Dancers and Musicians; Mikhail Baryshnikov, artistic director of the American Ballet Theatre; and Jerome Robbins, comaster and chief of the New York City Ballet.

improve the health and prolong the lives of those already suffering from HIV-related illnesses. The process of developing, testing, and distributing new medical treatments is long and slow. But there have been many advances in our understanding of how the virus works.

In February 1989, the Food and Drug Administration approved the use of a drug called aerosol pentamidine (AIR-uh-sohl pen-TAM-uh-deen). This medicine had been used for patients who were ill with pneumocystis carinii pneumonia (or "PCP"), an opportunistic disease that is often fatal. Now it may be used to prevent PCP from reappearing in people who had it previously.

Hospitals

The first hospital devoted entirely to the care of AIDS patients opened in Texas in 1987. It closed down within one year. The cost per patient was very high, and the medical-care costs could not be reimbursed. This raises a lot of questions. If the predictions come true, there will be approximately 270,000 people living with AIDS in 1991. They will need care and treatment. The present number of health-care workers and facilities isn't enough to handle the increased demand. To respond to the need for more AIDS care, we'll have to consider a wide range of possibilities.

Many people with AIDS have problems that can't be handled at home. They will need to be in a hospital or other care facility. People with severe pneumonia, for example, may need a respirator to help them breathe for days or even weeks at a time. Patients with cancer may need frequent chemotherapy treatments. Those with serious infections often need intensive medical care.

There will be approximately 270,000 people living with AIDS in 1991. They will need care and treatment.

Hospital administrators will have to decide how to handle the increased demands on their facilities. Some may find it necessary to add on to their buildings and create an entire section for AIDS care. Others may have to combine the care of AIDS patients with the care of other patients.

SHOULD PATIENTS WITH AIDS BE SEPARATED FROM OTHER PATIENTS?

There is much debate about the pros and cons of separating patients with AIDS-related illnesses from other patients. Health-care facilities will have to establish their own policies.

Keeping patients with AIDS together in one area would help protect them from getting illnesses and infections from other patients. Such illnesses and infections would burden their already weakened immune system.

Alon Reininger/Woodfin Camp

Keeping patients with AIDS together would also help build a support system. Patients with AIDS who share a unit can help each other by talking about common problems and individual solutions. Otherwise, people with AIDS might share a room with an uninfected person who is ignorant or prejudiced. This roommate might not know, for instance, that casual contact can't spread the virus. The person with AIDS might be afraid to talk to the roommate or to other patients, and vice versa.

Separating patients with AIDS-related illnesses from other patients also makes it easier to arrange for willing staff members to provide for their care. It might also help create an entire staff of people who would specialize in the care of patients with AIDS, as was done during the polio and tuberculosis epidemics.

On the other hand, separating patients with AIDS from the other hospital patients could have a negative effect. It might support the quarantine mentality. It might keep them from getting appropriate care if doctors, nurses, volunteer workers, maintenance workers, or visitors are reluctant to enter their rooms.

Other Care Facilities

Most people with HIV or AIDS don't need to be in a hospital, except for occasional stays of a few days or weeks. The rest of the time they could be home or at another kind of place where they can get care and treatment. Some need intermediate medical care (limited care in places like rehabilitation centers and nursing centers). The directors of such facilities are looking for ways to care both for those who are expected to recover from their HIV-related illness and for those who are expected to die from AIDS in the near future.

Other people with AIDS don't yet need hospital care or short-term care. But they will need a permanent residence where they can get medical care and support. There will probably be large numbers of infected people who are homeless. Some won't be able to afford to live in their homes if they lose their jobs. Others will be evicted from their apartments by fearful landlords, or because they are no longer able to pay the rent. Still others will be sent away by relatives who cannot or will not care for them.

There will also be an increased number of teenagers with HIV who aren't living in their parents' homes. Some will be on their own because of family problems. Others may be ordered by a judge to live in a group or foster home or in a residential treatment center. Boarding schools, colleges, and summer camps will have to learn how to accommodate HIV-infected adolescents. Sooner or later most of these places will have charge of a person with HIV or AIDS. These teens will need treatment and support.

The needs of all these infected people may transform our present social service centers into AIDS-care facilities. Nursing homes in your town may begin to make beds available for patients with AIDS. Many people with AIDS suffer a loss of mental functions in the final stages of the disease. So mental-health facilities will also have more patients with AIDS.

Many others become infected with HIV by engaging in illegal activities such as IV drug use. So the detention and prison systems will also have to deal with large numbers of HIV-infected teens and adults.

It won't kill you to spend time with
a friend who has AIDS.

Give him your support and compassion. He needs you.

Would you join a protest group that wanted him
to stay home?

→ Suppose your best friend told you she had
AIDS? Could you still be close friends with her?
Or would you start to avoid her?

What if you found out that the person who held this book before you had AIDS? Would you still hold it and read it? Or would you want to throw it away?

What you do, along with your family, friends, and community members, will directly affect the future course of the AIDS epidemic. The future will present situations that will challenge your belief in the facts. If you fall in love with a person who once used drugs, will you be able to talk about HIV? If you have sex, will you insist on safer-sex practices? If you hear that people with AIDS are staying in the nursing home where your grandmother lives, which group of protestors will you join—the one that wants them removed or the one that says that HIV-infected people deserve help and support? If a neighbor becomes ill with an AIDS-related disease, will you offer to bring him food and do some shopping? If someone with HIV infection in your school is being ridiculed, yelled at, or isolated, will you defend her right to be educated and respected?

Teenagers across the country are learning the facts about AIDS and doing something to fight the epidemic. Some teenagers in San Francisco had a rap song contest to help spread the truth about AIDS. Other teenagers in California have helped sew a giant quilt made of over 8,000 cloth panels. Each three-

Janet Woodcock

The AIDS memorial quilt, called the NAMES Project, on exhibit in Washington, D.C. The quilt has over 8,000 panels. Each three-foot-by-six-foot panel displays the name of someone who died from AIDS.

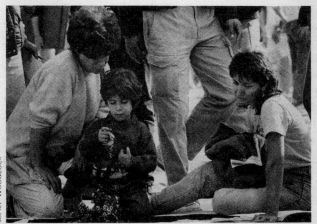

Janet Woodcock

Mourners at the AIDS memorial quilt.

foot-by-six-foot panel displays the name of a person who died from AIDS. The teens helped other volunteers keep track of donated fabric. They hemmed the cloth panels and helped sew names of the dead. They got involved in a project that will remind everyone who sees it that the people who die of AIDS are not just statistics. Each is a real person with a real name and a unique story.

Another AIDS project that relies on the volunteer help of teenagers is the Teen AIDS Hotline in Maryland. The hotline is run primarily by teenagers. They learn how to answer commonly asked questions by going to a seminar about AIDS and by asking each other questions. They keep up on the most recent information about HIV and AIDS by reading articles. These teenagers learn the details of the epidemic and at the same time share the information with everyone who calls for help.

You, too, can help in the fight against AIDS. Through your family, youth group, church, synagogue, or school, you might:

→ Set up or volunteer to work on a hotline for AIDS information.

→ Create a group to encourage discussion among your friends and classmates about the impact of AIDS and the HIV epidemic.

→ Organize a fundraiser (car wash, bake sale, magazine drive, etc.) to help support medical services, research, community services, and AIDS education.

→ Organize a debate to get facts and feelings out in the open.

Maude "Manny" Dull is a 17-year-old student at McAteer High School in San Francisco. Manny spends much of her free time as a volunteer, helping people with AIDS with such normal, day-to-day activities as cleaning, shopping, making appointments, talking, caring, and being a friend. She and other students like her are making a big difference in the lives of people with AIDS.

Overheard after school . . .

It's scary, thinking about AIDS.

Yeah, sure. But it's scary to go along pretending AIDS isn't out there, too! I'm glad we've been talking about it in school.

It's funny, but I think some things are changing around here. For one thing, Mickey stopped teasing me so much about being "Ms. Clean." You noticed?

I noticed. Maybe he decided playing it safe wasn't such a dumb idea.

It's the smartest move *I* ever made—and I don't plan to get dumber as I get older, either!

From *Teens & AIDS: Playing It Safe* (© 1987, 1988 American Council of Life Insurance and Health Insurance Association of America)

➔ Join a volunteer group that helps care for people with AIDS in your area.

➔ Organize a contest (rap or song, poster, bumper sticker, essay, etc.) with an AIDS prevention theme.

➔ Volunteer to review AIDS educational materials for use in your school or community.

➔ Talk about AIDS with your friends, parents, and teachers. Let them know your views and help them sort out the fears from the facts.

No one is sure about the future of the AIDS epidemic. But it *will* be a part of your life. Thousands of productive, creative, talented, and giving people will die before they have a chance to enjoy a full life. The epidemic will increasingly be the focus of political debates and proposed laws. You'll vote for the people who will make the laws and policies about AIDS. You'll live with concerns about HIV and AIDS in your neighborhoods and workplaces and families. What you know, what you feel, and what you do will affect how well you and others will live with the AIDS epidemic.

Call for Help:
A Resource Guide

This book contains the most up-to-date information available at this time. But to get the facts specific to you and your town, city, or state, you may need to contact someone who can answer your personal questions directly. Your teachers and counselors have information they can give you. Your family doctor can offer medical services and counseling. Your church or synagogue leaders can listen to your concerns and perhaps direct you to someone in your area who offers the services you need. But if you can't find the help you need, or you don't feel comfortable talking to people who know you and your family, this appendix lists resource centers that you can contact, by phone or by mail, to get help and information.

Hotline Phone Numbers

You can get more information about AIDS by calling any of the AIDS hotline numbers listed below. You don't have to give your name to the people who answer the phone, and in complete privacy you can talk to someone who will listen to your concerns, answer your personal questions, give you the name and number of a counseling and/or testing place in your area, and sometimes, if you ask, send you printed materials about AIDS.

Sometimes a hotline worker will ask you questions like "What state are you calling from?" or "How old are you?" These kinds of questions do not give away your identity; they are asked so the hotline center can keep statistics on who uses their service.

The telephone numbers that begin with 1–800 are toll-free (that is, they will not cost you any money), and if you dial these numbers they will not appear on your phone bill. There is a charge for the other numbers that are outside of your calling area, and the number you dial will appear on your phone bill. But if you look through the list, you will certainly find a contact that is either toll-free or close to where you live.

If you have trouble finding a listing for your area, call the National AIDS Hotline at 1–800–342–AIDS (that's 1–800–342–2437). The call is toll-free, and you can call 24 hours a day, seven days a week. The people at the hotline have a data base (computerized pool of information) of names and phone numbers for every area of the country. If you tell the hotline operator what area you live in and the type of information you're looking for—whether it's HIV counseling or testing centers, speakers for your school, drug treatment services for persons with AIDS, general AIDS information, even runaway assistance—the operator will tell you the numbers to call in your area.

AIDS Hotlines—National

AIDS Council of Northeast New York
1–518–445–AIDS (You can call collect.)

AIDS Hotline for Teens
1–800–234–TEEN
Hours: 4:00 P.M.–8:00 P.M. Monday–Saturday.
Staffed by trained high school students.

Brooklyn AIDS Task Force
1–718–638–AIDS (New York)
Hours: 9:00 A.M.–8:00 P.M. weekdays; 5:00 P.M.–
8:00 P.M. Saturdays; no Sunday hours.

Bronx Teen Pregnancy Network
1–212–585–7996 (New York)
(You can call collect.)
Hours: 9:00 A.M.–5:00 P.M. weekdays
Offers referrals to over 200 other New York City agencies.

Gay Men's Health Crisis
1–212–807–6655 (New York)
Hours: 10:00 A.M.–8:00 P.M. Monday–Thursday;
10:00 A.M.–6:00 P.M. Fridays; no weekend hours.

Hispanic Hotline
1–216–621–5696 (Ohio)

Long Island Association for AIDS Care, Inc.
1–516–385–AIDS (New York)

National AIDS Hotline
1–800–342–AIDS
Hours: 24 hours a day

National AIDS Hotline (in Spanish)
1–800–344–SIDA
Hours: 8:00 A.M.–2:00 A.M.

National Gay Task Force Crisis Line
1–800–221–7044
In New York call: 1–212–529–1604
Hours: 5:00 P.M.–10:00 P.M. weekdays;
1:00 P.M.–5:00 P.M. Saturdays.

**National Sexually Transmitted Diseases Hotline/
American Social Health Association**
1–800–227–8922
Hours: 8:00 A.M.–8:00 P.M. Monday–Friday.

Pediatric and Pregnancy AIDS Hotline
1–212–430–3333 (New York)
Hours: 24 hours a day

Philadelphia AIDS Task Force Hotline
1–215–232–8055
Hours: 11:00 A.M.–11:00 P.M. Monday–Friday;
3:00 P.M.–11:00 P.M. weekends.

AIDS Hotlines—State-by-State

In the following list, phone numbers that begin with 1–800 are toll-free, but can only be called from within that state. Telephone referral services for those states

Alabama	1–800–228–0469
Alaska	1–800–478–2437
Arizona*	1–800–342–2437
Arkansas	1–800–445–7720
California	
Northern	1–800–367–2437
Southern	1–800–922–2437
Colorado	1–303–331–8320
Connecticut*	1–800–342–2437
Delaware	1–800–422–0429
District of Columbia	1–202–332–2437
Florida	1–800–352–2437
Georgia	1–800–551–2728
Hawaii (Oahu)	1–808–922–1313
Idaho	1–208–345–2277
Illinois	1–800–243–2437
Indiana	1–800–848–2437
Iowa	1–800–532–3301
Kansas	1–800–232–0040
Kentucky	1–800–654–2437
Louisiana	1–800–992–4379
Maine	1–800–851–2437
Maryland	1–800–638–6252
Massachusetts	1–800–235–2331
Michigan	1–800–872–2437
Minnesota	1–800–248–2437
Mississippi	1–800–826–2961

listed with an asterisk (*) are provided by the National AIDS Hotline (800–342–AIDS). If you have trouble reaching the hotline operator for your state, call the National AIDS Hotline.

Missouri	1–800–533–2437
Montana	1–800–537–6187
Nebraska	1–800–782–2437
Nevada	1–702–885–4800
New Hampshire	1–800–872–8909
New Jersey	1–800–624–2377
New Mexico	1–800–545–2437
New York	1–800–541–2437
North Carolina	1–800–535–2437
North Dakota	1–800–472–2180
Ohio	1–800–332–2437
Oklahoma	1–800–522–9054
Oregon	1–800–777–2437
Pennsylvania	1–800–692–7254
Puerto Rico	1–809–765–1010
Rhode Island	1–401–277–6502
South Carolina	1–800–322–2437
South Dakota	1–800–592–1861
Tennessee	1–800–525–2437
Texas	1–800–248–1091
Utah	1–800–537–1046
Vermont	1–800–882–2437
Virgin Islands	1–809–773–1311
Virginia	1–800–533–4148
Washington	1–800–272–2437
West Virginia	1–800–642–8244
Wisconsin	1–800–334–2437
Wyoming	1–800–327–3577

Service Agencies

Agencies that provide AIDS-related services like education, counseling, and/or testing have been created in many cities across the country. Some of them are listed below. If you do not live near one of these agencies but need these kinds of services, there are four things you can do:

1. Call the National AIDS Hotline number listed above. The hotline can refer you to a service agency in your area.

2. Call one of the agencies listed below that can refer you to other agencies. Some of them will even let you call collect, so it won't cost you anything and the number won't appear on your phone bill.

3. Call Information (dial 411) and ask for the number of your state department of health. Call and ask them to refer you to a local AIDS information agency. This call may cost you money if the department is out of your calling area. If you don't want the phone number to appear on your phone bill, you can:

4. Call your town's board of health. They, too, should be able to refer you to the agency you need.

CALIFORNIA

AIDS Project Los Angeles
6721 Romaine Street
Hollywood, California 90038
1–213–876–8951
Hotlines: 1–213–876–AIDS (in Los Angeles County)
          1–800–922–AIDS (in Southern California)

1–800–222–SIDA (Spanish)
1–800–553–AIDS
(for the hearing-impaired)

This community-based organization provides a wide range of services, including counseling and support groups, buddy programs, insurance counseling, and dental and mental health care. Their Necessities of Life Program provides, to those with AIDS-related illnesses who meet certain criteria, free food and nutritional counseling, clothing and medical equipment, delivery services, and personal-care items. Their hours are 9:00 A.M.–11:00 P.M. Monday–Friday, and 9:00 A.M.–8:00 P.M. Saturday and Sunday.

Beach Area Community Health Center
Ciaccio Memorial Clinic
3705 Mission Boulevard
San Diego, California 92109
1–619–488–0644

This clinic provides counseling, screening, and a wide range of medical services. The clinic accepts all forms of insurance and will not turn anyone away because of an inability to pay. Their hours are 10:00 A.M.–6:00 P.M. Monday–Friday (call for an appointment).

San Francisco AIDS Foundation
25 Van Ness Avenue, Suite 660
San Francisco, California 94102
1–415–864–5855
Hotlines: 1–800–367–2437
(northern California only)
1–415–863–2437
(outside of northern California)

This foundation, with a staff pool of 600 volunteers, provides a wide range of educational, advocacy, and client services, including referrals for HIV testing and medical services, benefits and financial counseling, a food bank, an emergency-housing program, and general counseling services. All services are free and confidential. They will send printed materials free to anyone who requests them. Their hours are 9:00 A.M.–6:00 P.M. Monday–Friday. The hotline's hours are 9:00 A.M.–9:00 P.M. weekdays, and 11:00 A.M. –5:00 P.M. Saturday and Sunday.

Shanti Project
525 Howard Street
San Francisco, California 94105
1–415–777–2273

This group provides emotional and practical support for people with AIDS and their loved ones. Their services include counseling, medical referrals, recreation programs (tickets for events, trips, retreats, or parties), and a long-term residence program. All their services are free, except the housing program, which is based on one's ability to pay, and are fully confidential. The group has printed information that they will send free to anyone who requests it. Their hours are 9:00 A.M.–5:00 P.M. Monday–Friday.

FLORIDA

Health Crisis Network
P.O. Box 42–1280
Miami, Florida 33242–1280
1–305–634–4636

This agency offers confidential individual and group counseling for those addicted to drugs or alcohol. They have support groups and care partner groups, and they also offer counseling for the parents and children of addicted persons. Their youth program is open to Miami area youths ages 8–17. They are open 9:00 A.M.–5:00 P.M. weekdays.

GEORGIA

AID Atlanta
1132 West Peachtree NW
Atlanta, Georgia 30309–3624
1–404–872–0600

This program serves people with HIV or AIDS. It offers information, a buddy program, hospice programs, and referrals to medical services. It also trains teens to help other teens. These services are free and available to people of all ages from the metropolitan Atlanta area. The agency is open 8:30 A.M.–5:30 P.M. weekdays. They will send free printed information to anyone who requests it.

ILLINOIS

Sable/Scherer Clinic of Cook County Hospital
1835 West Harrison
Chicago, Illinois 60612
1–312–633–5182

This clinic serves Cook County residents of all ages. It offers confidential medical services, pre- and post-test counseling, a women's clinic, and bilingual services. These services are all free, but the clinic will take insurance payments if available. This clinic is open 9:00 A.M.–5:00 P.M. weekdays (no weekend service), and the women's clinic is open from 1:00 P.M. to 4:00 P.M. weekdays.

MASSACHUSETTS

Fenway Community Health Center
16 Haviland Street
Boston, Massachusetts 02115
1–617–267–7573

This center provides a complete range of services, including counseling, anonymous and confidential HIV testing, HIV outpatient treatment, and AIDS-related medical services. The center accepts all forms of insurance coverage and will not turn anyone away because of an inability to pay. Their hours are 9:00 A.M.–8:00 P.M. Monday–Thursday, 9:00 A.M.–5:00 P.M. Friday, and 10:00 A.M.–2:00 P.M. Saturday. The center will send printed materials free to anyone who requests them.

AIDS Action Committee
131 Clarendon Street
Boston, Massachusetts 02116
1–617–437–6200
1–617–356–7733 (hotline)

This AIDS service organization offers a wide range of extensive services, including a buddy program, meals, housing, and transportation programs, financial and rental assistance, and counseling and support groups. The organization will send printed materials free to anyone who requests them. Their hours are 9:00 A.M.

–9:00 P.M. Monday–Friday, 10:00 A.M.–4:00 P.M. Saturday, and 12 noon–4:00 P.M. Sunday.

NEW YORK

Adolescent AIDS Program
Montefiore Medical Center
Albert Einstein College of Medicine
111 East 210th Street
Bronx, New York 10467
1–212–920–2179

This is a special program set up to help youths ages 12–21 deal with the impact of the AIDS epidemic. The program offers complete medical evaluations, HIV testing, and pre- and post-test counseling. The services can be confidential, and the cost depends on your ability to pay. The program is available 9:00 A.M. –5:00 P.M. weekdays, and printed information is available free of charge to anyone who requests it.

Brooklyn AIDS Task Force
22 Chapel Street
Brooklyn, New York 11201
1–718–852–8042

This agency offers free AIDS information and support groups, and will set up buddy systems for people with AIDS from Brooklyn. It is open 9:00 A.M.–8:00 P.M. weekdays (on Mondays, services are available in Spanish, French, and Creole). There are no weekend hours.

Gay Men's Health Crisis
129 West 20th Street
New York, New York 10011
1–212–807–6664

This agency offers a variety of confidential services to gay men, people with HIV or AIDS, and their families. They have free printed information. They offer AIDS and nutrition counseling, legal services, and housing information, and they sponsor recreational and social events. They are open 10:00 A.M.–8:00 P.M. Monday–Thursday; 10:00 A.M.–6:00 P.M. Friday; there are no weekend hours.

Hemophilia Foundation
104 East 40th Street
New York, New York 10016
1–212–682–5510 (You can call collect.)

This organization gives free information about hemophilia and AIDS, referrals to other agencies, and support for hemophiliacs and their families and friends. They are open 9:00 A.M.–5:00 P.M. weekdays; there is an answering machine to take your message at other times of the day.

Hetrick-Martin Institute
401 West Street
New York, New York 10014
1–212–633–8920
1–212–633–8926 (for the hearing-impaired)

For youths ages 12–21 in the New York metropolitan area, this agency offers free confidential counseling, pre- and post-test counseling, HIV support groups, and after-school social activities for anyone who drops by. They are open 9:00 A.M.–8:00 P.M. weekdays. There are no weekend services. They will send free printed materials to anyone who requests them.

Mount Sinai Hospital Adolescent Health Center
Box 1005
19 East 101st Street
New York, New York 10029
1–212–241–7214
1–212–241–TEEN

This health center provides medical services, birth-control information and materials, and counseling, all specifically for adolescents ages 12½ to 21. Their services are confidential, and the cost will depend upon your ability to pay. (No one is refused services because of money problems.) They are open 9:00 A.M.–5:00 P.M. Monday–Friday. They have free printed materials that they will send to anyone who asks for them.

OHIO

Health Issues Task Force
2250 Euclid Avenue
Cleveland, Ohio 44115
1–216–621–0766

This AIDS service organization offers free counseling services, a buddy program, and financial assistance. These services are offered free, and the agency is open 9:00 A.M.–5:00 P.M. weekdays.

WASHINGTON, D.C.

Sexual Minority Youth Assistance League
1228 17th Street, N.W.
Washington, D.C. 20036
1–202–296–0221

This agency provides free AIDS information, counseling, prevention information, and social and support groups. These services are available to youths ages 12–21 who live in the Washington, D.C., area. This area includes metropolitan Washington, D.C.; Prince Georges and Montgomery counties in Maryland; and Fairfax, Arlington, and Alexandria in northern Virginia. The office is open 10:00 A.M.–6:00 P.M. Monday, Wednesday, and Friday; the youth groups meet from 12 noon to 3:00 P.M. every Saturday.

Help for Runaway and Homeless Teens

CALIFORNIA

Adolescent Treatment and Education Alliance
2751 Mary Street
La Crescenta, California 91214
1–818–248–2623

This adolescent AIDS service agency offers AIDS education services to youths ages 12–20. It provides a residential group home for HIV-infected teens 12–17 years old from Los Angeles County. This agency has people who train teens to teach other teens about AIDS, and also people who go out into the streets to give out information and bring back teens who want help.

Gay and Lesbian Adolescent Social Services (GLASS)
8235 Santa Monica Blvd., #214
West Hollywood, California 90046
1–213–656–5005

This agency provides a residential group home for adolescents 12–17 years old with HIV or AIDS. They offer free counseling, AIDS education, and referrals to medical centers for evaluation and testing. These social service workers go out into the streets every night from 8:00 P.M. until 2:00 A.M. to distribute survival kits that contain condoms, education materials, and hygiene products. They also offer youths ages 12–22 a safe place to stay. They have free printed material that they will send to anyone who requests it.

ILLINOIS

Neon Street
3227 North Sheffield
Chicago, Illinois 60657
1–312–528–7767

This is a program for homeless people ages 13–21. It offers AIDS education, support and counseling services, and sexuality and health education. It will give medical referrals for HIV testing sites. It is open 9:30 A.M.–8:30 P.M. seven days a week. Neon Street has free printed materials that it will send to anyone who asks for them.

NEW YORK

Covenant House
460 West 41st Street
New York, New York 10036
1–800–999–9999 (toll-free)
1–212–613–0300 (New York only)

Covenant House provides emergency services (shelter, food, clothing) and a variety of medical services for homeless and runaway youths up to 21 years old. Their services are free and confidential, and are available 24 hours a day. They have printed materials they can send free of charge to anyone who requests them.

The DOOR
127 6th Avenue
New York, New York 10013
1–212–941–9090

This organization offers confidential pre- and post-test counseling, HIV testing, and educational materials to runaway and homeless youths ages 12–21. Payment for these services can be made through Medicaid, Medicare, or private insurance. The services are given free of charge to those without insurance coverage. The DOOR has printed materials that it will send free of charge to anyone who asks for them.

Streetwise Project
Victim Services Agency
642 10th Avenue
New York, New York 10036
1–212–245–5140
1–212–619–6884 (24-hour runaway hotline)

This group provides food, counseling, AIDS education, and referrals for medical help and shelter for homeless and runaway youths up to 21 years old. Their services are free and confidential. From 1:00 P.M. to 12 midnight the outreach workers will travel anywhere in the city to meet teens who call for help. Weekend hours are 4:00 P.M.–12 midnight, and the runaway hotline is operated 24 hours a day, seven days a week.

Canadian Resources

AIDS Committee of Toronto
P.O. No. 55, Sta. F
Toronto, Ontario
Canada
1–416–924–5200 (Toronto only)
1–800–267–6600 (toll-free in Canada)

This organization offers free printed information about AIDS, and can refer callers to other agencies and services. They also operate a Deaf Outreach Program for the deaf and hearing-impaired. They are open from 10:00 A.M. to 5:00 P.M. and from 7:00 P.M. to 10:00 P.M. Monday–Friday.

Casey House Hospice
9 Huntley St.
Toronto, Ontario M4Y2K8
Canada
1–416–962–7600

This hospice organization, sponsored by the Ontario Ministry of Health, offers a variety of extended counseling, therapy, and legal assistance services to people with AIDS and their friends and families.

Ontario Ministry of Health
Public Health Branch
AIDS Section
15 Overlea Blvd.
Toronto, Ontario M4H1A9
Canada
1–800–267–7712

This hotline offers answers and referral services for the deaf and hearing-impaired within the Province of Ontario. The hotline is open 9:00 A.M.–5:00 P.M. Monday–Friday.

Glossary

Abstinence: The act of refraining from something—in this case, sexual intercourse.

AIDS: The letters stand for *a*cquired *i*mmune *d*eficiency *s*yndrome. It is the name for a certain group of illnesses that are all related to infection with HIV. AIDS involves changes in the body's immune and central nervous systems. These changes lead to a series of infections, cancers, or neurological problems that are hard to treat and may eventually cause death.

Anal intercourse: Sexual intercourse in which the male puts his penis in his partner's rectum.

Anonymous: Without any identification.

Antibody: A substance produced by the body to protect it against a foreign or unknown substance.

Antigen test: A test that looks directly for a virus—in this case, HIV.

Antiviral drug: A medicine that blocks the action of a virus (such as HIV) before it can do damage to other healthy cells or that stops a virus from multiplying within cells in the body.

Bisexual: A person who has sex with both males and females.

Body fluids: Any fluid found in the human body, such as blood, urine, saliva, sputum, tears, semen, and vaginal secretions. Only blood, semen, and vaginal secretions have been linked directly to the transmission of HIV.

Casual contact: Day-to-day interactions that might involve touching the outside of an infected person's body or touching the things that he or she touches. A list of examples of casual contacts is on pages 21–22.

Condom (rubber): A flexible shield that is placed over the penis during sexual intercourse. Its purpose is to act like a bag to collect semen and keep it from entering a sex partner's body. It also protects against transmitting the AIDS virus.

Confidential: Private or secret; containing information to be kept from anyone who does not need to know it.

Dementia: A loss of mental powers which affects a person's judgment and reasoning abilities.

Diaphragm: A molded rubber cap that fits inside the vagina and covers a woman's cervix. It is used to prevent pregnancy.

Ejaculation: The sudden discharge of semen from a man's penis.

ELISA: A test used to find HIV antibodies in samples of blood or tissues. The letters stand for *e*nzyme-*l*inked *i*mmu-no*s*orbent *a*ssay.

False-negative HIV test result: A test result in which the sample sent for analysis doesn't have enough antibodies or antigens present to be considered positive. This result implies that the person is not infected with the virus even though he or she really is.

False-positive HIV test result: A test result that indicates that the sample sent for analysis has enough antibodies or antigens present to be considered positive. This result implies that a person is infected with the virus even though he or she really is not.

Food and Drug Administration (FDA): A government agency that approves and licenses drugs for use in the United States.

Gay: A common name for a person who prefers sex with people of the same sex.

Hemophilia: A hereditary disease affecting males in which the blood does not clot as well as it should because it doesn't have enough of a component called Factor VIII (eight).

Heterosexual intercourse: Sexual intercourse between a male and a female.

High-risk person: A person whose behavior puts him or her at risk for being exposed to the virus that causes AIDS. High-risk behaviors include sharing needles and syringes during intravenous drug use, anal sex, and sexual intercourse with an infected IV drug user or an infected homosexual or bisexual male.

HIV: These letters stand for *h*uman *i*mmunodeficiency *v*irus. It is the latest name for the kind of virus that was first linked to AIDS. It used to be called HTLV-III, or LAV. Since there are several types of HIV, the one that is most commonly linked to AIDS is now called HIV-1.

HIV-2: A virus similar to HIV-1 that was found in West Africa in 1985. A few cases have been found in the United States. It may cause less serious illnesses than HIV-1, but it's still too early to be certain. Donated blood supplies in some parts of the United States are now being tested for this virus as well as for HIV-1.

Homosexual intercourse: Sexual relations between persons of the same sex.

Hospice: A program in which a team of health-care professionals works together to provide care for terminally ill people in their homes or in a special facility.

HTLV-1: A virus that has been linked to leukemia. It is found more often in Japan than in the United States.

Immune boosters: Medicines that strengthen the body's natural defensive response to infections or foreign particles.

Immune system: A system in the body that fights infection, diseases, and foreign substances.

Intravenous drugs: Drugs that are injected into the user's bloodstream, usually into a vein.

Junkie: A slang name for a drug user.

Kaposi's sarcoma: A previously rare form of skin cancer that often shows up as purple blotches on the skin. It is one of the cancers that people with AIDS may get. It is very difficult to treat.

Low-risk person: A person whose behavior does not put him or her at risk for being exposed to the virus that causes AIDS.

Mandatory testing: Testing that is required—in this case, for the AIDS virus.

Monogamous: Having a long-term sexual relationship with only one person.

Opportunistic diseases: Diseases that are rare in healthy people but that are often found in people with HIV infection. They commonly kill people with AIDS. They take advantage of the weakened immune system to get established in the person's body.

Oral sex: Sexual activity in which the male places his penis in his partner's mouth, or the woman's vaginal area is rubbed by her partner's tongue or mouth.

Organic brain damage: Harm to the brain cells or brain function that can result from HIV infection of the central nervous system.

Penis: A male's external sex organ. It contains the urethra—the tube through which urine and semen flow.

Pneumocystis carinii: A parasite causing a rare infection that usually settles in the lungs. It is an opportunistic disease that often causes pneumonia and sometimes death in people with AIDS.

Prevention: The act of stopping something—in this case, the spread of HIV and therefore AIDS.

Primary brain lymphoma: A rare cancer that starts in the brain. It is an opportunistic disease that often kills people with AIDS.

Quarantine: To isolate or to keep infected people separated from uninfected people, often against their will.

Rectum: The end of the intestines. It is through the rectum that a person passes bowel movements, or stools.

Routine testing: Testing that includes everyone in a particular situation—in this case, testing for the virus that causes AIDS.

Secondary infections: Common infections like mononucleosis (mono), tuberculosis (TB), and syphilis that often affect people with AIDS.

Semen: The fluid that is ejaculated from a male's penis when he has an orgasm—during, for example, sexual intercourse, a "wet" dream, or masturbation.

Sexual intercourse: A sexual activity in which the penis is put inside the vagina or rectum of another person.

Spermicide: A chemical product that stops sperm or other organisms like viruses or bacteria on contact. It is used as part of preventing pregnancy and some sexually transmitted diseases. It is most effective when used with a physical barrier like a condom.

Syringe: The hollow case that holds a drug or medicine before it is injected into a person's body.

Transfusion: The process of taking blood or blood products from one or several people and putting it or them into the body of another person.

Unprotected sex: Sexual intercourse without the use of a condom.

Vaccination: A medical treatment that protects people from getting a specific infection or disease.

Vagina: The part of the female genital tract that connects the uterus to the outside of the body. This is where the penis is placed during intercourse. It is also where a tampon is inserted.

Vaginal secretions: Body fluids that are found in a female's vagina.

Viral culture: A laboratory test that enables medical workers to grow a virus from the cells or body fluids of an infected person.

Western blot test: A test that is used to detect antibodies to HIV. It is more specific than the ELISA test, but it is more difficult to perform and more expensive. It is used to double-check blood, body fluids, or tissue samples that are found to be positive in ELISA testing.

Window period: A length of time in which a person is infected with HIV but has not produced enough antibodies to be found in tests of blood, body fluids, or tissues. The window period is usually from several weeks to six months.

"Works": The needle, syringe, and equipment used to mix and prepare drugs for illicit intravenous use.

Index